# MAKING LIVE MUSIC

## WRITTEN BY JOHN PEEL

additional material by
**Tom Robinson, David Anthony and Paul Quinn**

edited by **Paul Quinn**

design & production by ⌐

series covers by **Deni**

GW00730171

Many thanks to: Ken Achard, Gwen Alexander, Mark Bailey, Peter Barnard, Sharon Bird, John Burge, Mick Calvert, David Caulfield, David Coultas, Wally Evans, Graham Stockley, Andy Farmer, Justin Frost, Jerry Gilbert, Luke Giles, Dave Glover, Ginny Goudy, Keith Grant, Jay Green, Sean Hannam, Dennis Harburn, Keith Hardy, Sally Haseman, Gez Kahan, Dave Karlsen, Andy Lenthall, Mike Lethby, Gavin Mortimer, Paul Mulligan, Jason Newman, Carmel Parker, Nick Powell, Dave Rainger, Toni Rutherford, Michelle Smith, Mark Terry, Simon Turnbull, Bruno Wayte, Richard Wear, Sue Webb, Bob Wilson, Louise Wojnicki, Steve Wright, Steve Yelding and everyone else who helped.

*Making Live Music* is published by Nexus Media Ltd, Nexus House, Swanley, Kent BR8 8HY. Pre-press origination by Stirling Graphics, Southend, UK. Printing by Hastings Printing Company, E Sussex, UK. No part of this book may be reproduced in any form (except short extracts for review purposes) without written permission from the publishers.

## ISBN 1 872601 70 7

## FROM THE *MAKING MUSIC* LIBRARY

# HELLO CLEVELAND

Welcome to the none-more-public world of *Making Live Music*. The first time you take that step from practising or recording music at home, with only a mirror or the cat as a witness, to being in the spotlight (if you're lucky) on a stage, you need to be thinking about a lot more than just chords and notes. You have to consider things like pleasing, and keeping, an audience: in short, putting on a good show.

Whether it's the way you play, the way you sound, the way you put yourself across, or a combination of all these, there's got to be something about your live show that justifies *you* being on that stage as opposed to someone else. More fundamentally, there has to be something that makes an audience want to go to a live gig at all, rather than the cinema, or the video shop, or a club...

Live music took a battering in the late 1980s/early 1990s, but has staged a remarkable comeback recently. And it's not just down to the new generation of indie/rock bands either... the most successful and long-lasting dance acts are those who've recognised the entertainment value of a good live performance.

At the same time, the advent of CD quality live sound (and hi-tech visuals) at top concerts has raised audience's expectations. This doesn't mean you need to become a pro-audio boffin just to play a gig, but if you know a bit about sound (and lighting), and what can be done with it, you've got a head start.

That's where this book comes in. Written in no-nonsense, lay-person's language by an experienced sound engineer, with contributions from working musicians, it shines a torch into all those dimly lit areas of gigging and live sound, and prepares you for most on-stage eventualities.

We can't promise you'll end up performing at Wembley Stadium, but if you've got the raw talent and enthusiasm, we'll help you make the best of it. (And if you do make Wembley Stadium, we want to be on the guest list. Plus one.)

# CONTENTS

## SECTION THREE: CREATING YOUR SOUND

## SECTION FOUR: PRACTICAL GIGGING

# SECTION ONE
# THE
# BASICS

# A QUICK TOUR

While it's true the music and the way you play it are still the core of successful gigging, the technical tricks of the trade aren't exactly trivial items. Their effective use will help you communicate your tunes more, well, effectively to an audience – while their misuse could actually lose you that audience entirely.

Later in the book we'll look at your stage act and presentation, but first we'll talk about the gear you might use. In this chapter I'm going to introduce the main elements of the tech side of live music-making, along with some general thoughts about choosing your hardware...

## THE MAIN ELEMENTS

**Backline**: in case you haven't heard the term before, backline is the name for the amps and speakers you plug your guitar(s) and keyboard(s) into. (They're called backline because they're usually placed at the back of the stage – often, as chance would have it, in a line.)

As I'll repeat later (because it's important), the most fundamental point about backline is that it's every bit as crucial a part of creating your sound as your instrument itself. What works brilliantly for one musician and his/her style may be a total disaster for another.

**Microphones**: as with backline, your choice of mike can dramatically affect how your voice and/or instrument(s) sound out in punterland, so the vitally vital point is to try out any mike before buying. Also, bear in mind that a microphone can't adapt itself to you, so you have to adapt to it (see *Mike Technique*, later).

**PA**: there are really three items here – mixers, power amplifiers, and speakers.

To the uninitiated, almost any mixer can look horrendously complicated, simply because there are so many knobs and switches. Things aren't quite this bad in practice, because once you've mastered one channel, all the others are basically the same; but it's true that there are many types of features on mixers, and matching these to your own needs isn't quite the easiest game in town (which is why *Mixers* isn't exactly the shortest chapter in the book).

In introductory terms, there isn't really much that needs to be said about power amps – they either amplify your mix well, badly, blow a fuse, or explode. The first of these is generally the preferred option.

Speakers are quite interesting, because although the vast majority of models in semi-pro price territory look fairly similar and sport very similar features and tech specs, the sounds they produce can be very different. Again, it's a case of finding the one(s) that suit your music. Bear in mind that, whatever the brochure bumph may say, almost all budget and mid-price speakers are really only designed for vocals; models that can effectively handle, say, low bass, keyboards or drums, don't come cheap.

**Effects**: many guitarists will already be familiar with one or more effect types, but effects can also be incredibly useful on the PA side of things. Reverb, echo, compression, limiting, and enhancing can all increase musical communication, and though we're undoubtedly talking about mucho mazuma if you want loads of good quality effects, the really important point is that, whatever effects you're using, their musical effectiveness (as it were), can only ever be as good as the way you set them up. All those knobs and programs can thoroughly stuff your sound if you don't take the time to learn how to use them properly.

**Foldback**: most musicians like to be able to hear not only their own fluffs (usually audible via backline), but also those of their fellow-fluffers – so unless you're playing on a tiny stage, some kind of foldback/monitor system makes sense.

Many musicians like their monitors to play at appallingly loud levels (presumably as a result of the permanent hearing damage caused by years of listening to foldback at appallingly loud levels). Basic foldback, with just a few hundred watts, and two or three speakers all getting the same mix, isn't amazingly expensive, but if/when you get to the point of wanting separate mixes for each musician, then you're looking at more dosh than many bands can afford to spend on their main PA.

**Support systems**: no, not the friend who helps you stagger to the van post-gig, but all the bits and pieces that glue the bigger bits and pieces together and make them work (cables, distribution boards, stands and such). Main point here is that, though they may be physically small, if not always cheap, they're more than marginally material, because if they don't work, neither does the rest of your system. So I strongly recommend you take just as much care choosing them as the rest of your set-up.

# RELIABILITY, FEATURES, SOUND QUALITY and PRICE

These are the four main items you need to be concerned about when choosing any piece of equipment; I've listed them in the order I personally regard as most important, but I can well understand that, for many musicians, price is probably the first thing that matters. Trouble is, it's not a lot of good if you save money, only to find later that your chosen kit doesn't work when you need it to, doesn't have the features you really need, or doesn't deliver decent sound quality.

I think the bottom line here is that quality in any of these departments seldom comes cheap, so it's maybe better to wait and save a little (or a lot) longer, and get something that does the job properly. (There's the old saying that you only get what you pay for – in my experience, the more realistic version of this is that you seldom get what you don't pay for.)

If money's tight (which, as far as I know, is a situation most musicians have been in ever since they stopped receiving pocket money), then the first thing to sacrifice is features – for sure, you need the basic features to do the job, but it's all too easy to be tempted by extra gizmos and gimmicks, especially when they're being pushed at you by marketing and sales people. If you don't actually need it, leave it.

Reliability is something you can't easily assess when you read a brochure (have you ever known them say, 'This highly unreliable product'?), so all you can really do is rely on general brand reputation. Most current semi-pro kit is what I call 'fairly reliable'. Reliability isn't something you can see in an advert (as opposed to, say, the knobs, which you can), and the price-pressures of a competitive marketplace therefore mean the knob number-count generally comes before the knob quality-care (which is why totally top-line kit can easily cost three times a semi-pro equivalent).

Sound quality isn't quite so easy to sum up – on the one hand, it's probably not too surprising that a £200 mixer isn't likely to match the quality of a £20,000 desk; on the other hand, some budget kit can sound quite amazingly good (one reason being that cheap gear is usually electronically simpler, and most folk who know about this aspect of things agree that a simple signal path is a Good Thing). Also, in many cases, sound quality isn't about 'hi-fi' notions like fidelity, but about what works musically.

*All I want for Christmas is a 10k rig...*

## USING THE STUFF

Almost anyone can plug a few things together so sound comes out, but making the sound as good as possible, and keeping it that way, isn't so simple, which is where this book (fingers crossed) earns its keep.

Main point here is that it's not much good reading this magnificent manual if you don't then practise what it preaches – OK, so it'll take time before everything becomes second nature, and though this book is based on the personal (if not always totally professional) experience of musicians and engineers totalling well over 100 years between them, it can't cover every possible eventuality. But I hope it'll help you get to the gig, set your rig, live through the gig, and maybe survive to get home again afterwards (in close conjunction with your van manual, perhaps).

Anyhow, good luck and, above all, enjoy yourselves...

# POWER (AND SOME OTHER TECH-TALK)

There are loads of tech-type aspects to this audio lark, but most of them are only really of interest to pro engineers and anoraks. In this chapter I'm going to concentrate on those items the average gigging musician needs to have at least a nodding acquaintance with.

## WATTS, SOUND LEVELS and SPEAKER SENSITIVITY

As soon as you say power, most people think of watts. But it turns out there's a lot more to the subject than the simple idea that more watts always equal louder sound. The main concept to cover here is a little number called speaker sensitivity – this is all about how much sound you get out for the amount of power you put in.

Sound levels are normally measured with a special version of the dear ol' deciBel, called the dBA. We really don't need to go into precisely what a dBA is, which is probably Good News – suffice to say that background noise in a quiet living room is around 30 dBA, normal conversation 60-65 dBA, a noisy street about 90, and a typical pub band maybe 105-110 dBA (110 is when things could start to get painful).

Sensitivity is what dictates how efficient your speakers are at turning your amp's watts into sound – this is usually measured using a one watt signal and noting how much sound comes out one metre in front of the speaker (expressed as dBA 1W/1m). The higher the sensitivity figure, the better. Most hi-fi speaker models will produce 86-90 dbA on this test, while PA speakers will deliver anything from, say, 92 dBA up to as high as 102+ dBA.

This is Very Important Stuff, because the next item on the agenda is how sound levels increase as you up the wattage. If we start with one watt producing 92 dBA, two watts will deliver 95 dBA, four watts 98 dBA, eight watts 101, 16 watts 104, 32 watts 107, 64 watts 110, and so on (in other words, a 3 dBA increase corresponds to a doubling of the power).

There are two points here: how rapidly the power need increases for higher sound levels, and the fact that you apparently don't need all that much power anyway to get really high volumes.

If you consider that a pub band, including backline, vocal PA and drums, may effectively have a total of around 600 watts on tap, and you remember I said a moment ago that the very same band probably produces levels in the 105-110 dBA region, you might think my arithmetic's gone haywire somewhere along the line. It hasn't – the point is partly that, as I mentioned, sensitivity measurements are done with the sound level meter just a metre in front of the speaker, while audiences may be as much as, say, 15 metres away, and sound levels drop off dramatically with distance. The other aspect is that all those people, plus the furnishings, absorb a good deal of the sound.

Back to speaker sensitivity: remembering how the power need increases dramatically for higher sound levels, the range of sensitivity among different PA speakers becomes more than marginally important – a model with a 102 dBA sensitivity can hit 120 dBA with just over 60 watts, while a 92 dBA design will need 600 watts for the same level.

The point here is that amplifier watts don't come cheap, so high-sensitivity speakers could save you a not-so-small fortune on your amp budget. True, speaker sensitivity ain't exactly a free lunch either, but you'll generally find that a 3 dBA increase in sensitivity costs rather less than the equivalent doubling of amp power.

## AMPLIFIER POWER OUTPUT and SPEAKER POWER HANDLING

There are many ways of measuring power output, and some of them are, shall we say, just a little less realistic than others (this is how they can get away with marketing mumbo like £100 midi hi-fi systems boasting ratings of "100 watts total peak music power", which usually means the real output is something like five watts a channel).

Any remotely serious PA uses what are called RMS power ratings – these are a little more meaningful, but don't actually tell the whole story: a good amp will have the ability to work well above its official power rating for a few moments, and will also be able to deliver its rated

*JBL's new TR Series of PA enclosures offers the reliability of the JBL name at a budget price*

power hour after hour. Neither quality costs peanuts.

Of course, it's all very well having an amp with the power output of a small nuclear power station, but not much use if your speakers can't cope with the end-product. Trouble is, speaker power ratings are in some ways even more complicated than amplifier power.

There are three main rating methods in general use: continuous, peak, and music power. Continuous implies you can push the power into it for hours on end but, unless you're using drastically heavy compression/limiting, it doesn't generally mean too much in practice (it's often not made clear exactly how many hours on end it'll hold out); peak is the level above which you'll be looking into the joys of drive unit replacement after much more than just a few seconds (again, the number of seconds may vary); while music power is a moderately happy compromise between continuous and peak – though its real-world usefulness isn't totally dependable, since the quoted figure again depends on the designer's/marketing person's guesstimate of the dynamics of the music signals that'll be driving the speaker.

Different manufacturers can in fact often use the same descriptions to mean completely different things – if indeed they mean anything at all (see earlier "total peak music power" example). One standard that's becoming more widely accepted and may be worth looking out for is the AES (Audio Engineering Society), whose pink noise test specifies frequency bandwidths and duration of testing, making straight comparisons easier.

The bottom-line practical point is the game of matching amp output power with speaker power handling. Because of all the variables, it's simply not realistic to make hard and fast rules, but my own approach, on paper at least, is to aim for speakers with a music rating somewhere around the amp's continuous RMS rating. An infallible guide it's not, and there's certainly no need to bother if the ratings are 30-50 watts out either way, but it seems to work most of the time.

## LOUD ENOUGH?

Just over 30 years ago The Beatles were gigging football stadiums with only a few 50 watt amps (true, nobody could hear a note they played, but advanced sexual hysteria among the crowd meant it didn't matter). Today, it's not uncommon to find pub bands running somewhere between 500 and 1000 watts in small back rooms. So, if we temporarily set aside the not unimportant matter of the relationship between power, speaker sensitivity, and sound levels, how loud is loud enough?

This is actually a more than slightly difficult question to answer, but let's throw a couple of balls in the air:

First ball: whatever kind of volume level you're aiming for, the actual power you'll need depends on the size of the venue (the distance drop-off effect), and how many punters will be packed into it (the audience absorption effect).

Second ball: sound levels vary according to the style of music you're playing, and the kind of volume your punters want to hear it at. For example, even if we set aside the venue and audience size aspects, it's hopefully pretty obvious that semi-background music, even in a very large wine bar, is not going to need anything remotely like the same power as dance/techno music, even at a very small rave.

Taking the wine bar example, most of these venues exist primarily for the purpose of what might politely be called social intercourse, so you're unlikely to make yourself deeply popular if you play so loudly that asking the time results in being told, "Barcelona".

Even a large and noisy crowd will probably be quite adequately catered for with just a single 100 watt amp (I'm assuming we're talking about typical wine bar solo artists/duos, with just a couple of guitars/key-

*"Loud enough? Don't talk to me about loud enough. When I was a lad, the whole band, including the vocalist, plugged into one ten-watt combo." The Racketeers recreate the good old days on Brighton beach*

boards and maybe a drumbox, all running through the same amp).

At the other extreme, fans of heavy rock or rave music apparently have a sincere desire to experience long-term hearing damage; the music itself pretty much demands you use plenty of bass boost, or at least have the ability to cope with the already-boosted bass as on many dance/club mixes. Remember that using just 6dB of boost means you need four times the amplifier power you'd otherwise need.

Somewhere in the middle, we have the classic pub/club situation – but this in itself covers quite a variety of possibilities, mostly involving whether the audience is primarily there to listen to you, or get smashed while chatting with their friends.

Whatever the environment, there's a general point about sound levels, power and distortion. Speaking personally, I really and deeply hate having to suffer a PA system that's being pushed beyond its limits and into heavy distortion. OK, I know quite a lot of listeners do actually like their music distorted, but, in most cases, it's hard to argue that gross distortion does anything much to enhance musical communication.

# WATTS-PER-HEAD

Having taken a whole grab-bag of thoughts round the block, it's time to try to simplify things a little, and come up with something in the way of practical advice. And the advice here is what's called 'the watts-per-head guide'. Even this isn't quite as straightforward as you might like, but the general idea is that, depending on speaker sensitivity (we'll assume an average figure of around 95 dBA), the size and shape of the venue, the type of music, and how loud your audience wants to hear it, you should be aiming for a system that delivers a total of somewhere between two and six watts per member of the audience. The two watt figure might even be a little on the high side for the wine bar background example, but a bit of spare capacity makes sense for when/if you move up to playing a larger venue. A loud rock band or a rave disco could easily warrant the full six watt measure, while most pub/club scenes will get along quite happily with something around four watts.

Note, though, that I'm not talking about the power of the PA alone, but the combined output of PA, backline, and drums. Most backline is in the 30-100 watt range, while an average drum kit effectively contributes around 150 watts, so with a vocal PA that can musically balance against these (say 200-250 watts), you're looking at a typical total system power of about 500-600 watts. This is the kind of line-up you'd expect a semi-pro pub/club to have, and if the average pub audience is maybe 120 people, we're not far out from the four watt guideline.

Taking another example, if you're booked for Saturday night at the local cattlemarket, with a 400 capacity, and your normal bookings are in pubs, your usual system ain't likely to hack it very convincingly – so it's time to hire in a PA and run everything, except maybe drums, through it (backline will still be making its own contribution as well). In this instance, you'd be looking for a 1500-ish watt rig. This is right on the borderline for getting away without drum miking, so if you want a really powerful drum sound, you'll need to mike the kit – in which case, add another 500 watts, and be prepared to pay quite a bit more for the hire, with all the extra mikes involved and the time needed to set them up.

When it comes to playing open-air gigs, you need even more welly, because the sound you're making has nothing to contain it, and it disappears into the clear blue sky (or rain clouds, perhaps). Most semi-pro bands playing outside sound pretty naff because they haven't got enough power, and, if you don't want to fit into this category, make sure you hire the biggest rig you can get your hands on.

*Depending on circumstances, you should aim for a system that delivers between two and six watts per audience member. However, when you're playing in the open air, with nothing to contain the sound, the sky really is the limit. Hire the biggest rig you can get your hands on*

**19**

*All speakers have an impedance, measured in ohms – usually 4, 8 or 16 ohms. Impedance is a measure of the speaker's resistance, so the higher the impedance, the less power is delivered by the amp. Connecting speakers in series or parallel will affect the total impedance in radically different ways*

## SPEAKER IMPEDANCE, PARALLEL aND SERIES WIRING

Despite sounding fairly technical, these items are actually quite straightforward. All speakers have what's called an impedance, which is measured in ohms (the most common types being four, eight and 16 ohms). Fortunately, we don't need to bother about the theory behind all this, but there are some important practical points to consider – the first is that the greater the impedance (resistance) figure, the less power you get out. In theory, an amp should deliver twice as much power into four ohms as it does into eight – though it doesn't work out quite this simply in practice; it's usually about two thirds more. So an amp rated at, say, 300 watts into 8 ohms will produce about 500 watts into 4 ohms.

You have to be careful, though – most amps will operate happily into 4 ohms and above, but will object strongly (and probably expensively) to a lower impedance. Many PA speakers have outputs as well as inputs, enabling you to connect further speakers – this can be very useful, but, unless you're running very specialist kit, never connect more than one extra speaker. Two 8 ohm speakers running like this end up as a 4 ohm load, which just about any PA amp can cope with: two 4 ohm speakers combine to give a 2 ohm impedance, which isn't recommended.

## PHASE

Phase is first of all important with regard to microphones – it isn't usually a problem, but can be if you're running several mikes close together (as in miking a drum kit) and they're a mix of different brands (or of different vintages).

The problem arises because there's never been a standard agreement on how to wire XLR pins. It's not always easy to tell, but a warning sign is if you find, for example, that you lose tone on one drum when you bring up the fader on another – this is something you should spot at the *Creating Your Sound* stage (see Section Three). If it happens, go see your friendly local electronics engineer.

Speaker phase is important as soon as you have more than one speaker cabinet. The point about phase is that, if you get it wrong, one speaker cone will be pushing at the same time as another is pulling – this wastes power and messes up your sound (particularly at the bass end).

If you think you've got a problem, stick a single smack from the bass drum through the system, and you should be able to see the speaker cones moving in and out. If they're not moving in the same direction at the same time, then you have two remedies to choose from: either get the appropriate speaker wired the 'wrong' way round (which isn't too cool, as you'll almost certainly end up using the 'wrong' one(s) in the wrong place and end up where you started), or, preferably, get your local techie to change the wiring inside the offending cab(s).

## MONO AND STEREO

When you're playing live, you're already playing in stereo (unless you're playing such a small venue that the whole band is standing one on top of the other), but the idea of using stereo PA isn't necessarily all that sensible. The point here is that, although you can certainly have lots of stereo fun with effects like flangers, most of your music (particularly lead vocals, and anything with bass in it) really needs to go through both speakers.

One thing that can be said for stereo is that you've got two amps, so, if one goes down, you could get through the gig on the other. But then again, you might just as well carry a spare mono amp...

## SIGNAL LEVELS

You'll find quite a bit on this subject in *Mixers*. What I want to mention here is that there are two basic standards for connecting what are called 'line-level' signals (for example, keyboards and effects). One is the professional +4 dBU standard (don't worry about what a dBU is); the other is the semi-pro/amateur/domestic standard of -10 dBV. In theory, you can (just about) get away with running +4 kit into -10 inputs (though you risk overload distortion), while feeding -10 gear into +4 inputs increases background noise.

Most of the hardware you're likely to deal with will either be -10, or have both standards (usually in the form of -10 on jacks and +4 on XLRs, but sometimes switchable). If the levels are switched, check the switches are on the rear panel or somewhere equally accessible – it's a real pain if you have to take the lid off to move switches or jumpers.

## JACKS, XLRS and SPEAKONS

Try jumping up and down on an XLR for a while, and you'll get a very unhappy foot – do the same with a jack plug, and you'll get a very unhappy jack plug as well. Jacks also tend to come out of their sockets if you even look at them the wrong way, whereas XLRs usually have release catches. So, if you have a choice, it's XLRs every time. They're extremely tough stuff.

If you don't have that choice, and you're stuck with jacks, get into a routine of cleaning them every time you plug them in. There are well-made jacks, such as those by Neutrik, which will stand up to more abuse than the cheaper varieties, so they're ones to go for if you can – be warned, they'll cost you, but then few things good come cheap. Whatever you do, avoid jacks with plastic barrels – they break ludicrously easily, and they can be excellent sources of hum pick-up.

One thing to watch out for with XLRs is the pin wiring – most manufacturers wire them with what's called 'pin two hot', but there are a few variations, and, if you've checked every other possibilty for why a piece of equipment (especially a mike) isn't working, or you get phasey problems with drum mikes, it's worth having a look at the XLR socket wiring (or having someone who knows which end of a soldering iron gets hot to do it for you).

Speakons are a relatively recent arrival on the connector scene, and, as the name suggests, are designed exclusively for linking power amps and speakers. The enclosed plastic plugs, which comply with European safety guidelines, twist and lock into place – assuming both your amp and speakers are appropriately equipped. The marketing bumf tends to go on about how they're the best thing since sliced bread, but to my mind the most important benefit of Speakons over jacks and XLRs is simply that, because they're only used for power amps and speakers, there's no danger of someone plugging a mike into a power amp output – which doesn't do the mike a whole power of good  (and yes, it has been known to happen). Still, Speakons are almost bound to become the norm for speaker connections in Europe.

## FREQUENCY RESPONSE, NOISE and DISTORTION

Often called pitch, or a note, by musicians, frequency is measured in hertz and kilohertz (Hz and kHz), and the bigger the number of hertz, the higher the note. Real musical notes are actually made up of many frequencies (otherwise they would sound both boring and annoying), the lowest being called the fundamental and the higher bits the harmonics. Frequency response is about how a particular instrument, speaker, or system 'responds' along its frequency range.

Manufacturers go to lots of trouble to measure the noise levels and distortion figures of their kit, using irrelevant nonsense like sine waves, resistive loads, spectrum analysers, and oscilloscopes – the resulting numbers will be thrust at you when you're trying to choose your gear. Point here is that none of this means much, because the numbers simply don't relate to how equipment performs and sounds in the real world.

My advice is to use your own in-built measuring equipment, your ears, and trust them to tell you whether something is distorting, or not. After all, many guitarists use old valve amps to produce controlled distortion which actually improves their sound. If we call this musical distortion, and the other kind non-musical distortion, it's just a question of knowing which you like, and taking any figures with a pinch of salt.

# SECTION TWO
# HARDWARE

# MICROPHONES

It would be easy to say a microphone is simply a gizmo that turns sound into electricity, but unfortunately it would also be just a little less than the truth – there are quite a few tech-type aspects to consider, plus some more than marginally material musical matters to think about. We'll start with the tech stuff...

## BASIC TYPES –
## MOVING-COIL, ELECTRET and CONDENSER

Moving-coil mikes (also called dynamic) are the standard workhorses of live music-making. Their main virtues are that they're generally relatively cheap, potentially fairly good-sounding, and can be damn-near indestructible (as one of my musician friends constantly and boringly says, one of the best features of the legendary Shure SM58 is that, if need be, you can also use it as a hammer. This may, however, invalidate your guarantee).

Electret mikes have been around for about 20 years and, at their best, offer a kind of half-way house between moving-coils and the top-line condensers we'll discuss in a moment. Many early electrets earned the type a bad name, with problems like hiss, overload distortion, and susceptibility to damage by moisture (have you ever pondered how much liquid can pass between singer and mike during a two-hour gig?).

Good modern electrets have largely overcome these problems, but it's unlikely you'd choose one as a vocal mike – their main advantage over moving-coils is a potential for greater subtlety/finesse, and this is usually only a significant plus-point for instrument miking, especially with cymbals.

All electrets need a power supply – on cheap models this is provided by a battery, which is somewhat less than Good News for day-to-day gigging, since Sod's Law dictates the battery will die somewhere in the middle of the second set. More expensive models offer the choice of battery or phantom-powering (see *Mixers*), but budget PAs seldom offer phantom facilities. My own opinion is that, though a good electret may be great for home recording, it simply isn't relevant to most gigging work, at least until you get to the stage of full drum kit miking.

Condenser mikes are, without doubt, the Rolls-Royce of the biz, a fact that's usually reflected in their price tags. Their main benefit is potentially superb and unbeatable sound quality in almost every application, but their downside is that, rather like fine wines, they don't necessarily travel well: road- and roadie-proof they may, in principle, be – but that really depends on the road and the roadie.

Still, if you're in the market for £300+ mikes, chances are you've got the kind of roadie who'll know how to look after this kind of kit. Condensers require phantom-powering, but it's unlikely you'd be considering them if you didn't have a mixer with this feature. Current buzzword with condensers is 'large-diaphragm', which is not a method of contraception, but a feature associated with delivering a warm, 'intimate' sound – this is most-often mentioned in connection with vocal work, but could be applicable to almost anything, especially guitar miking.

## PICK-UP PATTERNS –
## CARDIOID, HYPER-CARDIOID and OMNI

Pick-up patterns have nothing to do with chat-up lines (at least not in this particular book). A cardioid pattern simply means that a mike is most sensitive to sounds coming from directly in front of it, rather less so to sounds from the sides, and least of all to sounds from behind the direction it's pointing in. (You've probably seen those 'heart-shaped' pick-up diagrams, where you have to imagine the microphone pointing into the indent at the top). This makes a lot of sense for live work, since in most cases the PA speakers the mike is feeding will either be to one side, or nearer the audience (which more or less counts as being behind the mike's front-end), so feedback is minimised.

Note that some brands call cardioid mikes uni-directional, which may be a convenient marketing term, but maybe stretches the meaning of 'uni' (ie one) just a weeny bit beyond reality.

Hyper-cardioids, as you might guess, are even more directional than cardioids – in theory at least. In practice, there are wide variations, and quite a few cardioids have 'tighter' directional qualities than some hypers. It's also worth noting that, depending on your PA layout, hypers are generally slightly worse at rejecting sounds coming from directly behind them.

Omni-directional mikes (omni = all) are equally sensitive to sounds from any direction. Used appropriately, this makes them great for, say, miking a whole string section with just a single mike. But since you very possibly don't have an eight-player string section in your band (and if you do, you'll probably be able to afford individual miking), they're not muchly relevant to most gigging musicians – especially because their lack of directional discrimination makes them very prone to feedback problems. Still, just thought I should mention them, so you know to avoid them.

Moving from tech to musical matters, the important point with pick-up patterns is not, in many cases, about the extra directionality of hypers over cardioids, but more to do with the different kind of sound 'character' the two types can create. This is hard to put well into words, but it's often said that a hyper somehow reaches 'deeper' into the sound it's miking – which maybe makes sense, as you're getting more of the direct sound, and less of the ambience that surrounds it. Whether or not this is something you want, only you can decide, but, depending on the specific mikes in question, we're definitely talking different 'flavours'.

## PROXIMITY EFFECT

This is a very important aspect of all cardioids and hypers, and simply means that, as sound-source and mike get closer, the bass end of the frequency range gets boosted. To some extent, this can be a Good Thing, since a degree of added warmth can be attractive, especially on vocals, but by the time you get so close that the mike could catch herpes, it often becomes excessive. There's no way of avoiding this, as it's part of the nature of cardioid/hyper design, but models do vary in the extent of the feature/problem, so it's something to think about and check out when you're choosing a mike. (See also *Mike Technique*.)

## BUHS, PUHS, ESSES and EFFS

Yesh, looksh like the typesetter had an excessively large liquid lunch, but we're actually talking about explosive and sibilant consonants – little items that can actually pose quite major problems when you use a mike for vocals. What happens is that Bs and Ps tend to acquire a nasty 'blasting'/'popping' effect, while Ss sometimes come out as a kind of 'tchssy' sound, and a surprising number of mikes have problems with Fs, making them sound somehow 'furry'. These effects are at their worst when you sing really close to a mike, and also rather depend on the character of the vocalist's voice, but some models handle the problems better than others – which is just one more reason for really checking out a mike before you actually commit to buying it.

## APPLICATION TYPES –
### VOCAL, INSTRUMENT, GENERAL-PURPOSE, SPECIALIST aNd CLIPS

Vocal mikes have two particular tonal qualities that set them apart from other types: their bass is rolled-off (reduced), to lessen the proximity effect, and they have a 'peak' in the upper-mid/lower-treble region to increase clarity and help voices cut through the rest of what's going on – this is often called presence, because it makes your presence more, er, present.

Instrument mikes, in theory at least, have a much flatter frequency response, while some designs seemingly try to have their cake and eat it, by calling themselves general-purpose – which I guess means they have a bit of bass roll-off (but not much), and a bit of a presence peak (but not much). Personally, I wouldn't bother too much about these distinctions, because though there are some mikes that only work well in certain applications, most decent mikes can do a credible job with pretty much anything they're shoved in front of (I know one guitarist who insists on his cab being miked with an SM58, and sod the fact that it's officially for vocals).

Among mikes intended for specific jobs, the best-known example is probably the Shure Green Bullet used for harmonicas, and reputedly developed from the intercom mikes Shure made for World War II American tanks. There's no doubt the Bullet gives loads of presence, but overall I don't actually find it better than most vocal mikes for the purpose, simply because the latter generally give better detail, and the presence peak can fairly easily be simulated with a decent mid-sweep EQ on the mixer (see *Mixers*).

I must admit I'm not a great fan of specialist mikes in general, mostly because there's a small-to-serious price premium over 'normal' models – but if you like the sound a particular design produces, and can afford the additional ackers, then don't let me put you off.

Probably the most widely-used type of specialist mike is the clip-on, which has two main applications: drums and brass/wind instruments. The major attraction for drum miking is that conventional mikes need piles of stands that not only cost considerable crinkly, but can also be a real pain to set up when you're in a rush/short of space. The drawback of clips for drums is that they only pick up the sound from the edge of a drum, and that isn't necessarily the sound you're looking for. Convenience versus flexibility. May be fine for live use, but I can't think of a single pro studio that uses clip-ons in preference to conventional miking – then again, pro studios don't generally have time/space problems to contend with. By all means try 'em, and if you like the results, buy 'em.

I also have reservations about using clip-ons with brass and wind instruments. The attraction here is that it's in the nature of saxing that player and instrument are going to wander around quite a bit, which, with ordinary miking, inevitably results in considerable level and tonal changes.

To some extent, the former can be solved by the sensible use of a compressor, but the tonal change aspect isn't quite so simple. For example, many sax-maniacs actually like the expressive effects they can create by using conventional miking as part of their playing technique (give 'em plenty of foldback, so they can hear what's coming out), while others are quite happy with the consistent sound a clip-on gives, preferring instead to use their playing technique to create the expression they want. It's horses for courses.

## RADIO MIKES

Once the exclusive preserve of big-name, big-money artists, radio mike prices have plummeted dramatically in recent years, to the point where you can now get a decent rig with something like an SM58 head/capsule for well under £300.

The most important thing about radio mike systems is that there are two basic types, known as single and diversity receivers. Single designs have just one aerial to pick up the transmission from the mike, and are very prone to interference and signal loss; diversity types have two aerials and receiver front-ends, plus a monitoring circuit that constantly checks reception quality from both aerials, and automatically switches between them to get the best results. Even though the two aerials are only a foot or so apart, this generally makes a world of difference to the reliability of performance and, quite frankly, I wouldn't even con-

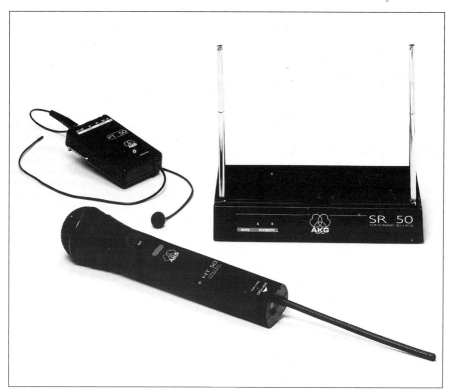

*Radio microphone systems like this*
*AKG WMS 50 are no longer the sole*
*preserve of superstars*

sider buying a single receiver type, especially as the price difference is now only about £30-40.

(The type of diversity receiver I've described should technically be called a 'true' diversity system, because there used to be a diversity system that had two aerials but only one front-end. As far as I'm aware, these aren't made any more, and most 'true' diversity types are now just called diversities, but you might conceivably come across one of the old designs in the second-hand market – they're nowhere near as good as 'true' diversities.)

Further points about radio mikes are that, because of all the extra circuitry involved, you can't reasonably expect to get sound quality that's quite as good as with a cabled system. But, with decent designs, the difference isn't likely to be enough to lose sleep over.

Also, the old and infamous problem of interference from other users (well-known vocal line, 'Anyone pick up a fare from the Queen's Head in ten minutes?'), is now largely a thing of the past, following changes in the frequencies used – something to check up on though, if you should happen to consider buying a second-hand set-up. There have also been problems in the past with radio mikes occupying "illegal" frequencies, though most now have (or are seeking) authorisation from the Department of Trade & Industry (DTI).

Bear in mind too that frequencies vary from one country to another, so if you're likely to be touring abroad, be sure to buy a model that can have its frequencies changed easily and cheaply (usually by the importers). There's currently a bit of confusion on this subject, because as from early 1996, there's a common EC standard for the type-approval of radio mikes: quite a few people apparently think this means all radio mikes will use the same frequencies – it doesn't, and mikes will still need their frequencies to be changed for use in different countries.

Final point: radio systems don't have to be used only with vocal microphones, or indeed, with mikes at all – in principle at least, you can use them with pretty much any instrument. This could well make sense if, for example, you're using a clip-on mike with a sax, since you lose the restriction and visual distraction of a trailing cable. But if you think about radio-miking a guitar, it's only going to work sensibly if your effects run through the effect/insert loop(s) of your backline amp – if you're still physically plugged into footpedals, then a radio system is a fairly pointless idea.

## HEAD-WORN MIKES

Most-commonly used by drummists (and gymnastic singers), their attractions are considerable: many skin-smackers move their heads around considerably (quite often you can hear the bits inside rattling), so conventionally-miked pick-up of their vocal contribution is going to suffer from fairly massive variations in level. What's more, providing foldback in earpieces is far easier (and on big gigs, cheaper) than by rows of high-powered monitor amps and speakers.

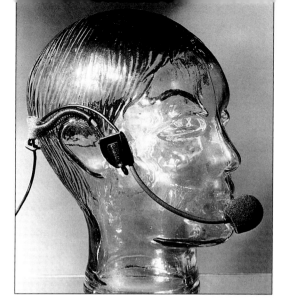

*Microphone headsets can seem like a very practical solution for the more gymnastic performer, but despite micro-technology, they're still far from visually discreet*

I'm not convinced about their suitability for vocalists, despite the recent trend (probably started by Kate Bush, and taken up by the likes of Peter Gabriel, Madonna and Take That). Despite the micro-technology, head-sets are still far from being visually discreet: this could count as a bonus in image terms (like maybe in techno/dance music), but does run the risk of making you look rather pretentious, or at least less human – more like a NASA flight controller or switchboard operator than a musician.

Performance-wise, there's the undoubted practicality on the fold-back side – in-ear monitoring gives singers full freedom of movement and both hands free – but, as with clip-ons for instruments, you lose the ability to vary mike distance and angle as part of musical expressiveness.

Some up-market theatre productions now tackle the problem of mobile vocalists by using tiny (and very expensive) omnidirectional mikes pinned to the singer's head. Again, though, while the quality's far better than you might think, sound control is limited, it's not immune to knocking or blocking, and, close-up, it does look a bit odd. Besides which, it's probably way beyond your budget.

## MUSICAL MUSINGS

The fundamental point here is that, as I said a while back, a microphone is not a simple item: a mike that may be magic with one singer, or for miking one particular instrument, may sound absolutely awful under different circumstances. So it pays to take your time over choosing the mike that's right for you. Fortunately, many dealers now offer 'hire-for-a-day' or 'sale-or-return' facilities, and these give you the opportunity to take any serious contender(s) round the block in real-world conditions.

Also, the sound a mike delivers will vary quite considerably, not only according to the distance it's placed from the sound-source, but also as you alter its angle in relation to said source (watch how some of the real pros use these qualities to their musical advantage). These are aspects you have to experiment with − bearing in mind the basic principle that you have to adapt to the mike, because the mike can't adapt to you.

# SELECTED MICROPHONES
## − EXAMPLES OF CURRENT MODELS

(This list is not intended to be comprehensive,
or to recommend some models above others)

There are literally hundreds of mikes competing for your custom, at prices from £20-ish to well over £2000. Nobody could claim to have tried every mike in every application, so all I can do is pick a few I've had experience with, and reckon are above par for their price.

(Prices quoted in the book are current recommended retail, inc VAT.)

### SHURE BETA GREEN BG 1.0 − £46
One of Shure's recent budget successes, it produces a rather dry, slightly light sound (a common Shure trait), but rates as fine value for money.

### STUDIOMASTER KM 81 − £70
Despite some buh/puh problems, it produces a bigger, warmer sound than the BG 1.0, and the price difference is not as great as it might seem, since the 81 comes with a decent quality cable, which must be worth a tenner in its own right. The cheaper though identical-looking KM 51 delivers a much hollower sound.

*Shure's Betagreen family (above) includes the BG1.0 (left) which, at just £46, represents great value for those on a tight budget, while Beyer's M300 TG (below) is a popular alternative to the classic SM58*

### AUDIO-TECHNICA MIDNIGHT BLUES MB 3000L – £94

Somehow managing to combine a slightly warm overall balance with distinct toppiness (which might or might not be a prob depending on whom/what you're using it with), I find this to be a stormer for the dosh.

### BEYER M300 TG – £116

Long-running SM58 look-alike, I must admit I've had something of a soft spot for this mike for several years. Warmish balance, moderate detail, it's just a mike that works well, and most people like.

*Left: Robust, balanced, with no vices – Shure's classic SM58 and SM58S;
Right: AKG's D 3800 – above average performance justifies extra cost*

## SHURE SM58 – £150

Thirty-plus years old, and still going strong. There are other mikes around this price that score more highly in one area or another, but the 58's great virtue is that it's a robust and balanced performer with no vices worth talking about. (The newer, upgraded Beta 58 is £229.)

## AKG TRI-POWER D 3800 – £186

Well above average in just about every area, this is the first mike I've met that can seriously claim to justify its slight price premium over the 58. Check it out.

Other brands worth trying out, depending on your finances, include Byetone (budget Russian successor to the revolutionary Oktava dynamics), Peavey, Spirit, Yamaha, Sennheiser, ElectroVoice...

# MIXERS

If you go into a panic at the sight of row upon baffling row of knobs and faders, this is where we'll try to break it all down into understandable chunks for you. True, it's a subject that could get very complicated, partly because of the vast variety of features on different mixers, but also because different mixer manufacturers offer different mixes of these features. There's also a world of difference between the facilities you're likely to find on a £300 mixer-amp and those on a £1000+ desk...

So, rather than demolish a small rain-forest exploring every single nook and cranny (or knob and socket), plus their many potential permutations, I'm going to concentrate on what I think are the important fundamentals, then take a look at how they fit together to create a mixer that, hopefully, meets your needs.

## INPUTS

There are really just two basic kinds of input: mike and line. Mike inputs will usually have XLR sockets (on better mixers, at least); lines generally use jacks. Mike inputs are almost always what's called balanced, which means there are three wires inside each cable - two to carry the signal, and the third to provide protective 'screening' against interference pick-up from mains and other nasties.

Line inputs may be balanced or unbalanced, the latter using just two wires - this makes them much more prone to interference problems, but as line inputs usually work at higher signal levels, it doesn't generally matter too much in practice, unless you're running really long cables (say over 30 feet).

It's also relevant to point out that, even on the mid and up-market desks with balanced line-ins, these may not count for much, because though you can quite happily plug an unbalanced source into a balanced input, you only get the benefits of balancing if the signal source is also balanced; and almost all backline, keyboards and semi-pro effects have unbalanced outputs.

Once you get beyond the cheapest hardware, you can expect to find items like a trim/gain control - this is a Good Thing, partly because it matches the strength of the incoming signal to the mixer electronics, reducing the risk of overload distortion, but also because it allows you to use the full travel of the channel's main volume control for fine-tuning the mix, rather than having to fiddle with tiny adjustments at one or t'other end of the scale. On some desks, trim only works on the mike ins, but it's quite handy if it works on the lines too. You might also find a pad switch, which simply cuts the incoming signal's strength - handy in cases like miking a bass drum.

On desks from £400-ish and up, you'll probably have phantom powering as a mike input option. This is used for condenser mikes, and supplies the juice they need to run. On top-line mixers, the power will be switchable on each channel, but most semi-pro desks have 'global' phantom switching, and this could lead to problems: it's OK to run phantom into a non-condenser mike, or indeed any source, so long as it's balanced, but Very Bad News if whatever's connected to the input is an unbalanced source, which could lead to blown fuses (inconvenient) and/or equipment damage (expensive).

Most unbalanced sources are line-level, and you'll fairly bankably avoid the potential prob if you only ever connect such kit with jack leads, so you can't accidentally plug them into the phantomed XLRs. The rare, but important, exception case is if you happen to be running a low-output guitar straight into your mixer (ie without going through backline or effects) - if the line in doesn't have enough gain, you'd be tempted to use a mike input, but since guitar outputs (except on specially customised pro jobs) are unbalanced, you'd be inviting disaster. The only answer is to buy a DI box (see *Accessories*).

## EQ (EQUALISATION)

EQ/tone controls come in many different flavours, but the basic point is that the more flexible it is, the more useful it can be. Not surprisingly, the more you pay, the more flexible the EQ tends to be.

Simplest of all is two-band bass and treble - which isn't entirely useless, since it allows a degree of overall tone-shaping, but nothing much beyond that.

First step up is three-band, which adds a mid-range boost/cut control. This definitely adds more flexibility, but not an awful lot, because simple reality says that the bass, mid and treble frequencies available

*The more flexible the EQ is on a mixer, the more useful it is*

may not be those you want to work on. Enter sweep EQ...

The basic concept of sweep is that you add a second control to the basic boost/cut knob; this second knob allows you to vary or sweep the frequencies it affects over a range. The most typical example is mid-range sweep - while a basic mid might typically have its 'centre' frequency somewhere around 1kHz, a sweep will probably have a range of 250Hz to 5kHz - the numbers don't matter much, but the tonal control it gives you does, as it allows you to tune in to the frequencies you want to work on. Sweep is neat.

Beyond basic sweep, we get into all sorts of variations on the EQ themes: bass and treble controls may have switchable frequencies (for example, 6/12kHz for treble), and you may find two overlapping sweeps, one covering mid-bass to upper mid-range, the second going from lower mid-range to where the treble control takes over. Experienced PA mix engineers generally value two sweeps very highly indeed, partly because a single sweep doesn't generally go low enough to hit the frequencies that most often need fine-tuning, especially on vocals, and an ordinary bass control is too crude a tool to do the job really effectively, while having an upper sweep as well is useful for controlling the degree of presence/cut through.

Sweep is not the same as full parametric EQ, normally found on more up-market mixers: true parametric EQ has an extra control - the Q - which lets you select the exact width of frequencies affected either side of your chosen 'centre'. Very useful, but rarely found on anything less than pro gear.

Possibly the simplest but most useful EQ facility is a low-cut/bass roll-off filter switch - this can be brilliant for reducing 'buh'/'puh' problems with vocal miking, and also pick-up of general stage rumble and mush. In fact, I'll go so far as to say I find it very difficult to take seriously any mixer intended for live work that doesn't offer this feature. Using bass EQ cut to do the job is no substitute, because it also, and usually unwantedly, affects upper-bass and lower-mid-band.

One other facility worth mentioning is an EQ in/out switch, which is a fine idea in principle, but needs using with considerable care. The point here is that, by the very nature of the beast, EQ changes overall levels, and it's a well-established fact that, all other things being equal, louder always sounds better. So, whether you're using additive (boost) or subtractive (cut) EQ, any comparative in/out judgements you make may be influenced by the level change as well as by the actual EQ. No easy answers to this one but, hopefully, forewarned is forearmed.

## EFFECT AND FOLDBACK SENDS

Whether you're sending signals to an outboard effect such as reverb, or feeding a foldback/stage monitor rig, it's very possible that you'll want a different mix of the various ingredients from that feeding the main PA. (Common examples include having much less reverb on bass guitar than lead vocals, or giving the drummer a far higher level of bass than in the main mix or other players' foldback.)

Effect and foldback sends allow you to create these different mixes, and come in two main flavours: pre- and post-fader. Pre-fader means the send levels are not affected by changes to the main mix, and is most-commonly used for foldback; post-fader is generally used to drive effects, so changes in the mix are reflected in the amount of effect treatment the various sources receive.

Budget PA, such as all-in-one mixer-amps, may have only one or two sends, and this should be fine for most users, because if you're only running 200-300 watts, typically for vocals, you probably won't need any stage monitors, and a single send will cover your reverb/echo needs. But once you get to the stage of running the whole band through the PA, foldback becomes pretty much a necessity, and you'll almost certainly find that just a single mix will be a compromise that satisfies nobody. This means, thinking ahead, you should really be looking for a desk with enough foldback sends to give every bandmember their own mix.

One extra feature to look for on both effect and foldback sends is a master level control - this isn't essential, because most effect units and power amps have their own input level controls, but it's generally more convenient to be able to control things from the desk.

## EFFECT RETURNS

As you'd imagine, these are used to bring the effected signals back into the mix. On basic PA, there'll probably be nothing more than a level control, but what's important is that, even though the PA may be mono, the return input needs to be stereo, simply because almost all modern reverb/echo units have stereo outputs. Quite a few budget PAs fail on this count.

With more expensive kit, you can expect several returns, and these may have their own EQ, usually simple two-band. You can of course use main inputs as returns, which may offer more EQ flexibility, though you

have to be very careful not to turn up the relevant sends on such channels, or you'll get a fairly unhealthy dose of the dreaded feedback (stick
a large dollop of BluTack completely over the relevant knobs).

If you're using stage monitors, it's extremely desirable to be able to
feed the effect returns into the monitor mix - this is easy if you're using
main channels for the return inputs, and a surprising number of budget
PAs offer simple return-to-monitor switching - on the other hand, a surprising number of fairly expensive desks lack this facility, so it's something to watch out for.

## GROUPS/BUSSES

With low-cost PA, the channels all feed straight into the master level
control, which is quite adequate for the kind of jobs they're usually
used for. But as you move up-market, you start to have the option of
desks that allow channels to be grouped together before they get to the
main level fader.

This can be very useful if you're at the stage of, for example, drum
miking, or running several keyboards without their own sub-mixer,
because having spent time getting the 'internal' drum or keyboard balance right, it's a real pain if you then decide you want the drums/key-
boards as a whole to be a bit louder/quieter. Without groups you have to
readjust every channel - which pretty much guarantees you'll lose your
carefully-created internal balance - whereas with groups you just
push/pull the appropriate group fader(s).

Many musicians also use their mixers for home studio recording,
and group facilities can be invaluable here, at both the track-laying and
mixdown stages (the usefulness in the former application depends on
whether or not you're running several sources to a single tape track).

The downside of groups is that they do add substantially to the
cost of a mixer. Generalising both wildly and dangerously, I'd say that a
four-group desk will meet most bands' needs, and if you think you need
more, it might be cheaper to look at a separate sub-mixer for sources
such as keyboards.

The abbreviated description of mixers (eg 16:8:2) usually gives the
number of channels first, then the number of groups/busses, and then
the number of outputs.

*Above: new Spirit Folio SX portable mixer, and, right: close up of a single Folio channel strip*

## INSERTS

Not to be confused with channel inputs, inserts are the equivalent of backline effect loops, and provide a simple way of patching an effect into just a single channel or group. Inserts normally use a stereo (three-pole) jack, which needs a 'splitter' adaptor to enable separate cables to be connected to the effect's input and output. Inserts are good, and unless you're buying on the tightest imaginable budget, or doing all the work they might be used for via backline loops, I wouldn't even consider a mixer without them.

## SOLO

The idea of a solo button is you can listen (usually during your sound-check, or on cans/headphones mid-gig) to just a single channel, group or effect, without altering the main mix(es). This is handy for tracking down problems like hum or distortion, the source of which can otherwise take quite a while to locate, and would involve disturbing your mix. Look for 'latching'/'locking' solo switches, because without them you can't engage solo and then potter off to find and fix the cause of the naughtiness.

## METERING

The simplest, and single most useful, form of metering is just an overload/'clip' LED that tells you when you're approaching distortionsville. They're not totally dependable when used as an indicator of power levels, because they don't usually reflect how the amp is handling the actual speaker load it's driving, but they're a lot better than nothing.

Multi-LED 'ladder' meters are fun to watch, but I have to say I find most of them rather annoying, because though they're good at indicating how close to overload you're running, and give an impression of the dynamics of signals, they don't generally go low enough. Most designs only show levels down to around -20 dB, whereas I like meters that show levels as low as -60, so you can easily see background noise and hum nasties.

Probably the most important point about metering is that, as you get into mid and up-market mixer territory, the meters need to have switching that enables you to display what's happening in just about any part of the system (individual channels, groups, et cetera, often via solos), rather than just the main outputs.

## MONITORING

Rather like metering, a monitoring section is really only as useful as the flexibility it provides in selecting what it is you're monitoring. Main problem is that most live monitoring has to be done on cans, and I've not yet found a single moderately-priced desk that provides remotely enough level to drive cans to the kind of volume you need to hear anything above the sound levels the band is likely to be chucking out. To some extent, you can get round this by using the high-sensitivity in-ear cans sold for use with personal stereos - unless your budget stretches to a proper in-ear monitoring set-up; otherwise the solution is to connect the monitor section to a budget hi-fi amp, which should be able to kick ass sufficiently.

## ERGONOMICS/FEEL

This is a vast subject, the bottom line being that you can have every feature in town, but if the desk isn't easy to 'drive', you're going to find it a pain in the posterior in practice.

For example, some mixers have their connectors round the back rather than on top, and the latter is a damn sight easier and quicker to set up and patch into. EQ with centre (flat) detents is good, especially if there isn't an EQ in/out switch. Look for control knobs with meaningfully-coloured endcaps, and buttons that make it easy to see whether they're up or down (a common failing on many desks).

Channels, groups, and even effect returns should have a panel where you can write, or stick a label describing what they're being used for. On any mixer that has proper metering, the faders should be calibrated in dBs rather than from 0-10, so when you see a channel or a level running, say, 3dB too high, you know exactly how much to pull the relevant fader. Bear in mind too that a desk which looks great in the bright lights of a dealer's showroom could be a very different proposition in the stygian gloom of a typical pub/club, and though the problem is easily solved with a gooseneck/anglepoise lamp, you probably don't really want to bring the mixer to the audience's attention.

## PUTTING IT ALL TOGETHER

Down in budget territory, cost constraints mean most mixers offer fairly similar features, which is usually fine, because such desks are generally used for basic vocal mixing.

Once you get to the stage of running backline, keyboards, other instruments (say brass, wind or strings), and drums through the main PA, then it pays to spend as much time as possible working out your mixing needs - then wading through manufacturers' bumf to make a shortlist of candidate desks. If funds permit, bear in mind that your needs may well change over time, so extra channels, sends and such like, could save you the financial pain of future upgrading.

I've already mentioned the value of sub-mixers for applications like keyboards, and there are many reasonably-priced models; a further advantage is that the sub-mixer can be located next to the keyboards, allowing the player to fine-tune his/her mix while tickling the ivories.

On the sound quality front, most desks deliver results that, though hardly the last word in audio subtlety and sophistication, are entirely adequate at the jobs they're intended for. Reliability is not such a happy story, though, and I think you'll find many pro engineers will agree that even £1000+ desks often show problems (noisy faders and such) after as little as a year or two's hard work.

The basic point here is that (as mentioned earlier) competition between brands is largely based on providing the maximum number of features at any given price-point, and since true-pro quality components can easily cost three times their domestic equivalents, you're not really likely to get what you're not paying for. This is another good reason to buy a mixer with at least a couple of extra channels, so you'll still be in business when the odd channel dies in the middle of a gig.

# SELECTED MIXERS

## EXAMPLES OF CURRENT MODELS

(This list is not intended to be comprehensive,
or to recommend some models above others)

*Mixer prices (and sizes) have come down dramatically:
Samson's MixPad 9 offers 9 channels for just £199 (see below)*

### SAMSON MIXPAD 9 – £199

✦ Three mike/line inputs, three stereo inputs (total of nine channels)
✦ Two auxiliary sends per channel for greater flexibility
✦ Two stereo effects returns
✦ Independent two-band EQ
✦ Phantom-powered XLR mike inputs
✦ Adjustable mike input trims
✦ Balanced stereo output

## SPIRIT FOLIO LITE – £320

✦ 12 inputs with a maximum of 16 available at mixdown
✦ Inserts available on all mono inputs and mix outs
✦ Pre Fade Listen Solo on all inputs
✦ Four dedicated stereo inputs
✦ Switchable phantom powering
✦ Dedicated stereo and tape returns
✦ Separate stereo outputs for tape, monitors and headphones

## STUDIOMASTER DIAMOND CLUB 8/2 – £338

✦ Eight balanced XLR mike and jack line inputs
✦ Switchable phantom power
✦ Three-band EQ
✦ Two post & two pre-fade aux sends
✦ PFL, clip LED
✦ Balanced XLR left, right and monitor outputs
✦ 12 LED output bargraphs

## SOUNDTRACS TOPAZ MINI – £351

✦ Four mono and four stereo inputs
✦ Phantom power on mike inputs
✦ Three-band fixed EQ on mono inputs, two-band on stereo
✦ Two independent aux sends
✦ Two dual-operation ten-segment bargraph meters
✦ Two stereo effects returns with level controls

## MACKIE MS1202-VLZ – £399

✦ 12 inputs – 'Very Low Impedence' circuitry
✦ XLR mike inputs with phantom power
✦ Mike/line input levels
✦ Four balanced/unbalanced mono inputs and four stereo inputs
✦ Tape inputs and outputs
✦ Two-band EQ
✦ Switchable three-way LED peak meters
✦ Two aux sends per channel and two stereo effects (aux) returns

# IF YOU'VE GOT IT, FLAUNT IT.

Don't keep your talent hidden. Get it upfront where it'll get noticed, with Celestion's CR Series. They won't let you down on stage. A range of hard working, professional loudspeakers that are big on sound and utterly reliable.

They won't let you down on the road, either. Rigid construction, protected corners and toughened grilles make CR ideal for a bit of hard rocking. And of course, the best sound in the business.

Make the most of what you've got. It's show business, after all.

Celestion International Ltd., Foxhall Road, Ipswich, Suffolk, IP3 8JP. England. Tel: 01473 322222. Fax: 01473 729662.
Celestion Industries Inc., 89 Doug Brown Way, Holliston, MA 01746, USA. Tel: 508 429 6706. Fax: 508 429 2426.

**CELESTION**

# 3 THINGS MAKE OUR NEW POWERED MIXER STAND OUT

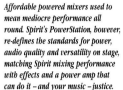

*Affordable powered mixers used to mean mediocre performance all round. Spirit's PowerStation, however, re-defines the standards for power, audio quality and versatility on stage, matching Spirit mixing performance with effects and a power amp that can do it – and your music – justice.*

With PowerStation Graham Blyth has excelled himself: there's a new pre-amp design that will take any signal you care to throw at it, plus a subsonic filter across the output to tackle speaker speaker rumble without stopping you using bass EQ. The on-board digital effects are by Lexicon - the choice of large studios around the world. Even the power amp is an audiophile's dream, really meeting its specifications to deliver 300 watts (peak) per side of pure Spirit sound*. So what's missing? Just the hiss, muddy reverb and distortion that you'd expect to find on a powered mixer at this price. These, on the other hand, are just a few of the features that you *will* find on PowerStation:

### Bullet-Proof Mic Pre-Amps
With gain ranging from 0 to 60dB Graham's new **UltraMic™** pre-amps gives you even more signal handling capacity to connect signals ranging from low output dynamic mics to active DI boxes without fear of clipping. Just as important, at -129dBu EIN their noise performance exceeds that of many so-called professional mixers.

### High Pass and Subsonic Filters
A new no-nonsense 100Hz High Pass Filter with an 18dB/octave cut-off means you can tackle low frequency rumble more effectively. A 40Hz subsonic filter across the outputs lets you create bass-heavy mixes without overloading PA cabs with frequencies they just can't handle.

### Mono and Stereo Inputs
We've given you two full-spec stereo line input channels in addition to the 8 mono mic/line channels – ideal for keyboards and samplers. The stereo effects return and 2-track tape return can also be used as stereo inputs.

### LEX Appeal
Lexicon effects have pride of place in the effects racks of studios around the world. A carefully chosen range of breathtaking effects algorithms adds a final polish to your music.

### The British Sound
Everyone knows British EQ is the best. PowerStation's mono inputs use Graham's acclaimed *3-band EQ with swept mid.* Impedance-balanced outputs and electronically-balanced inputs – especially important in electronically hostile stage environments – keep the audio clean going in and out of PowerStation.

### 7-Band Graphic EQ
Simple graphics will not solve feedback problems: to isolate the 'ring' at exact frequencies really needs at least 27 very steep, close-spaced filters. Instead, PowerStation's graphic EQ has been designed as a *creative* tool to give you a brilliant sound whatever the room acoustics.

### The Right Controls, for Real Control
Custom fader laws give PowerStation's new 60mm channel faders smooth, predictable response, and a full 100dB of attenuation – so you get *complete silence* when you fade out. Custom-designed controls provide an even spread of gain and smooth response.

### Channel and Master Inserts
A good live sound is often helped by external EQ and dynamics processing – channel and master inserts take care of that.

*\* 265 watts RMS x 2, continuous into 4Ω*

### Flexible Auxiliary Routing
Aux 2 can either be routed internally or to an external processor. Aux 1 is switchable pre/post fade, for pre-EQ stage monitoring or more effects.

### Patchbay
The comprehensive patchbay lets you bypass the power amp to drive a bigger PA, feed another mixer into the power amp, or even route external signals (or the aux outputs) through the graphic EQ.

### Power Amp
Most powered mixers deserve their reputation for using poor quality power amps. Not so PowerStation, whose 300 watts (peak) per side amp* offers both audiophile performance and enough power to blow your socks off. We can guarantee this amp doesn't just meet spec, it *exceeds* it.

### Rugged Good Looks
PowerStation is built like a tank. Period. A hinged cover protects the mixer from beer, dust and roving hands that shouldn't be playing with your knobs. Rack ears are available too for rackmount use.

**Spirit by Soundcraft™**
Harman International Industries Ltd.,
Cranborne House, Cranborne Industrial
Estate, Cranborne Road, Potters Bar,
Herts., EN6 3JN, England.
Tel: +44 (0)1707 665000
Fax: +44 (0)1707 665461

**SPIRIT** By Soundcraft

**H** A Harman International Company

### y Compromise?
Spirit we believe that quality esn't have to carry a price emium. However, designing werStation gave Spirit's sign guru, Graham Blyth, eater challenges than mere ordability. In 25 years of xer design Graham had ered clear of low-cost wered mixers, because he dn't want to be associated th the terrible reputation any had for poor audio and ild quality. However, when : told him that PowerStation d to be a tool that audio-iles would be proud of he on changed his mind! Read to find out how he signed a console that es you performance, wer and change in ur pocket.

## YAMAHA MM1402 – £429

✦ 14 inputs – six mono, four stereo; two outputs
✦ Mono channels have XLRs (with phantom power) & 1/4in balanced jacks for line level; three-band EQ, gain and pan; two aux sends, one pre & one post fade
✦ Stereo channels have 1/4in jacks on stereo channels, with switchable line level, two-band EQ, one aux send, and balance
✦ All inputs channels have PFL solo switches
✦ Stereo sub input for second sub-mixer or stereo instrument
✦ Five-band graphic EQ in master section
✦ LED bargraph meters for stereo buss
✦ Dedicated tape in/out

## SPIRIT FOLIO 12/2 – £446

✦ Eight mono inputs, two stereo inputs
✦ XLR and jack inputs on all mono channels
✦ Three-band EQ with swept mid on mono ins
✦ Two-band EQ on stereo ins
✦ High Pass Filter
✦ Dedicated tape return
✦ Momentary soloing on inputs and aux masters
✦ Insert points on output masters
✦ 12-segment bargraph meter
✦ Also available as rack-mount

## SOUNDTRACS TOPAZ MACRO – £468

✦ Ten mono and two stereo inputs
✦ Phantom power on mike inputs
✦ Three-band fixed EQ on mono inputs, two-band on stereo
✦ Two independent aux sends
✦ Two dual-operation ten-segment bargraph meters
✦ Two stereo effects returns with level controls

## PEAVEY UNITY 2002 (12-channel) – £519

✦ 12 balanced XLR mike and unbalanced jack line inputs
✦ Switchable phantom power

**Crest Audio presents the V and Vs series. Amplifiers designed to deliver all your music-always. Earth-shaking bass and effortless mids and highs come from generous power reserves. Fail-safe protection and road-tested reliability keep you in business, night after night, year after year. All created by the makers of the world's leading concert sound amplifiers. About to rock? Power up at your local Crest Audio dealer.**

# for those about to rock

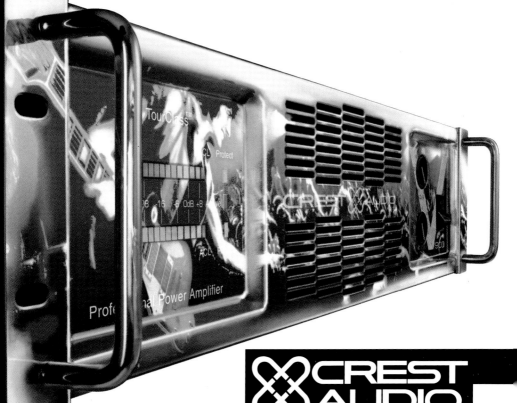

*Peavey Unity 2002 features four ten-segment LED bargraphs*

✦ Three-band EQ
✦ Dual Monitor and FX sends
✦ Dual master controls
✦ Stereo tape in/out with level control
✦ Four ten-segment LED bargraphs for main & monitor outputs

## YAMAHA MX200 (8-chANNEl) – £599

✦ Eight channel live/general purpose mixer
✦ Selectable A/B XLR and jack inputs, plus channel inserts
✦ Phantom power on XLRs
✦ Three-band EQ on all channels
✦ Four aux sends on all channels (two pre, two post fader)
✦ Left and right stereo and mono output busses
✦ On/off and PFL solo switches on all channels
✦ Switchable 80Hz high-pass filter to cut live hum and rumble
✦ Two stereo returns, with two-band EQ, plus tape in/out
✦ Four ten-segment LED bargraph meters

## SPIRIT FOLIO SX – £611

✦ 20 inputs (12 mono/four stereo); eight direct outputs (pre or post fade), two sub-busses, and dedicated mono out

54

- ✦ UltraMic input pre-amps allow any mike/line device to be used
- ✦ Three-band EQ with swept mid and low bands and high pass filter
- ✦ Three auxiliary sends (two pre or post fade)
- ✦ Freestanding frame, with carrying handle

## SPIRIT LIVE 3 Mk2 8/3 – £868

- ✦ Eight inputs, three outputs
- ✦ Additional mono buss with separate fader
- ✦ Extra-quiet UltraMic+ pre-amps
- ✦ Four-band EQ with two swept mid bands and high pass filter
- ✦ EQ bypass switch
- ✦ Four aux sends (three pre or post fade), and four stereo FX returns with EQ "slope" control
- ✦ -20dBV record output
- ✦ Eight channel expander available

## 3G MYNAH PLUS 16/4/3 + HUSH – £881

- ✦ Ten mike inputs, 16 line inputs (total of up to 24 inputs at mixdown)
- ✦ Four sub groups
- ✦ Up to nine different output mixes
- ✦ Two independent HUSH noise reduction circuits, to clean up noisy input or output signals, and gate empty channels
- ✦ 19in rackmount unit

## SPIRIT FOLIO RAC PAC – £925

- ✦ Up to 28 inputs at mixdown
- ✦ Pre-Fade Listen or true Solo-in-Place monitoring
- ✦ Send any channel signal to a direct output or route it to a group
- ✦ Three-band EQ with swept mid and High Pass Filter
- ✦ Free-standing design with built-in rack ears
- ✦ Connector fields on rear of console can be repositioned on underside

## STUDIOMASTER SESSION-MIX GOLD – £936

- ✦ 16/2 PA mixer
- ✦ Three-band EQ with swept mid
- ✦ XLR mike inputs with phantom power

*Yamaha's MX200 offers selectable jack/XLR inputs (see previous page)*

◆ Inserts and four aux sends (two pre, two post fader) on all channels
◆ Two mono and two stereo aux returns with pan and level controls
◆ Channel on/off and solo functions
◆ Two twin-band EQs, switchable from outputs to aux returns 1&2
◆ Tape input and output phono sockets
◆ 12-segment bargraph meters

## YAMAHA MX400 (8-channel) – £999

◆ Up to 16 inputs – eight mono, four stereo
◆ All mono and two stereo channels have XLR and 1/4in connectors
◆ Switchable phantom power
◆ Inserts, on/off switches, plus signal & peak indicators on all inputs
◆ Three-band EQ on all channels, with sweepable mid
◆ Five aux sends: two pre-fade, two pre or post
◆ Mono and stereo input signals assignable to four-group and stereo output busses
◆ Six assignable 11-segment bargraph level meters

## SPIRIT FOLIO 4 – £1209

◆ 20/4/2 console for live and recording work
◆ True four-buss group section routeable to the mix
◆ Four stereo inputs with switchable two-band EQ

- ✦ Choice of six busses from inputs
- ✦ Eight aux sends, dedicated tape send and return and monitor out
- ✦ Four dedicated stereo returns
- ✦ Two 12-segment stereo bargraph meters
- ✦ Line-up oscillator and headphone jack

*Spirit Folio Rac Pac: a free-standing design with built-in rack ears*

## ALLEN & HEATH GL2 – £1291

- ✦ 18/4/2/1 rackmounting console
- ✦ Four groups
- ✦ Four-band EQ with low and high swept mid frequencies
- ✦ Stereo and mono outputs
- ✦ Ten mono inputs and two stereo inputs
- ✦ Four stereo returns
- ✦ XLR mike inputs with individually switchable phantom power

## SPIRIT LIVE 4 Mark II – £1532

- ✦ Four-buss live/recording console
- ✦ 12 mono plus two stereo inputs
- ✦ Four-band EQ with two swept mids

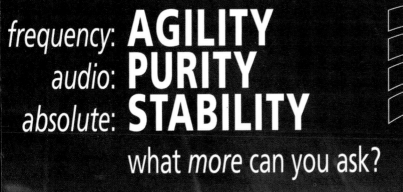

◆ Direct outputs on all channels
◆ 6x2 matrix provides two extra discrete outputs
◆ Dual Stereo inputs with linear faders and EQ
◆ Insert points on input groups and master sections
◆ Six auxiliary sends – four can be pre or post-fade
◆ Four stereo returns for effects
◆ Eight channel expander available

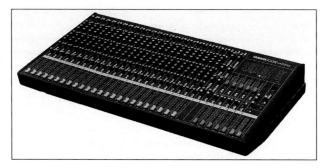

*Yamaha MX400: up to 16 inputs and switchable phantom power*

## STUDIOMASTER SHOWMIX – £1899

◆ 16/4/2 PA mixer
◆ XLR mike inputs with individually switchable phantom power
◆ Four-band EQ with two swept mid frequencies
◆ Six aux busses (four post, two pre fader)
◆ Four stereo aux returns
◆ 16-segment LED meters with dedicated peak-reading PFL meter
◆ Insert points on inputs, subgroups, and outputs
◆ Two-band EQ on outputs

## SOUNDTRACS MAXI 24 – £1939

◆ 24/4/2 PA mixer
◆ 20 mono and two stereo inputs
◆ Unique switching set-up converts from four to eight-group output
◆ Four-band EQ with low and high swept mid frequencies
◆ Eight aux sends
◆ Master section with monitoring and talkback facilities
◆ Fader automation package available for PC Windows

**The seal of real quality.** From first to last, simple to highly complex, Clay Paky and Pulsar products are widely considered the very best in their categories. But Clay Paky and Pulsar also mean much more - from twenty years of professionalism to an endless list of technical firsts and market successes, a history of promises that have always been kept, the support of the best retailers and thousands of satisfied customers worldwide. This is what makes Clay Paky and Pulsar a Team to rely on, to ensure you are making a real investment in your future.

*Allen & Heath's GL2: XLR mike inputs with individual phantom power*

## YAMAHA PROFESSIONAL MIXER 01 – £1999

✦ 16/2 digital mixer
✦ 16 input channels with gain trim & pad (8 balanced XLR, 8 jack)
✦ Three-band parametric EQ on inputs, FX returns and stereo outputs
✦ Cue function for solo of input channels and aux sends
✦ Four aux sends, two for internal effects, two for external
✦ Stereo input channel
✦ Stereo, Record and Monitor outputs
✦ Analogue two-track in/out for stereo recorder
✦ Four fader groups
✦ Motorised faders
✦ 33-position pan control
✦ Large backlit LCD display
✦ 12-segment stereo LED meters
✦ MIDI functions
✦ Two digital multi-FX units and three dynamic processors built-in

## ALLEN & HEATH GL3 – £2231

✦ 16/4/2/1 front-of-house or monitor mixer
✦ Four groups
✦ Top-mounted connectors for easy access
✦ Four-band EQ with low and high swept mid frequencies
✦ Six aux outputs
✦ Four group outputs with sub-grouping to stereo
✦ Ten mono inputs and two stereo inputs
✦ Four stereo returns
✦ XLR mike inputs with individual, switchable phantom power

# POWER AMPLIFIERS

Although the combined mixer-amps we'll be looking at in a couple of chapters have many attractions, mostly for smallish-scale (typically vocal) PA at budget-to-mid prices, once you get to running general PA (with or without drums), separate mixers and power amps have considerable advantages. Not least of these is that even top-line mixer-amps don't tend to be all that powerful (even stereo models seldom deliver much more than 250 + 250 watts, which isn't really enough for any but the very smallest general PA needs). In this case, you might, not unreasonably, ask, why run general PA at all?

Most people tend to think of power amps as little more than simple 'black boxes' – you shove a fairly low voltage signal in, and out comes a fairly large dose of watts. But though power amps are indeed a lot simpler than most other PA components, they're not quite that simple – so here's the lowdown...

## POWER

We already covered this in some detail in *Power (And Some Other Tech Talk)*, but the practical point here is to think very carefully indeed about how much power you actually need, not just for the kind of gigs you're currently playing, but for the larger venues you'll (maybe) be playing before too long. Even without drum miking, I really can't see much point in going for anything below 300 watts a channel, while 600+ watts a side makes a lot more sense (remembering that 600 watts only delivers sound levels 3 dBA higher than a 300 watt jobbie, and 3 dBA isn't an awful lot, subjectively). With drums as well, you almost certainly need at least 1000 watts a channel. Amps in this power range don't generally look cheap on paper, but their prices start to make more sense when you break them down into pounds per watt (or watts per pound).

## INPUTS

Very straightforward: only the cheapest power amps have jacks as their sole inputs, while mid-price models usually have both jacks and XLRs, the latter being vastly preferable. Volume/gain controls are useful, because they allow you to set the running level so the mixer's meters actually relate (more or less) to how hard you're driving the amp(s) – look for controls that don't move too easily, so they're less likely to get disturbed during transport and set-up.

## OUTPUTS

There are two main types of output on most amps: speakers and slaves. Speaker outputs use jacks on budget amps (even bare-wire binding posts on hi-fi type amps), XLRs on some more expensive models, while an increasing proportion of mid and top-end models use Neutrik Speakon connectors (yet again, see *Power (And All That Stuff)*).

Slave outputs are used for feeding extra power amps without the need for using splitter adaptors back at the mixer. You might not consider them a particularly useful feature right now, but they could be very handy if you get to the stage of playing larger venues that need more powerful amping.

Note that slave outputs on power amps are a line-level signal, and cannot themselves drive speakers, unlike the external speaker sockets on some backline and PA speakers, which are occasionally labelled 'slave' (presumably in an attempt to confuse us all).

## METERS

Most of what you need to know about metering is in the *Mixers* chapter, but here are a few thoughts that apply particularly to power amps. The single most useful meter is just a single LED that comes on when the amp is getting close to running out of power/into overload distortion. After that, another very useful meter is a 'signal present' LED, which can be a Godsend if you hit major probs, because then you know how far the signal is getting/not getting in your chain. A very valuable LED is one which shows if the protection circuitry has cut in. Speaking of which...

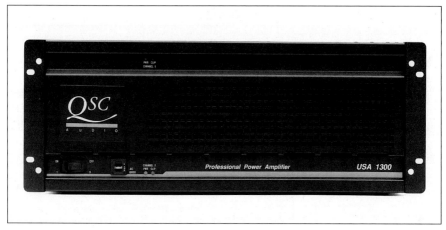

*Comprehensive protection circuitry is a feature of the QSC USA 1300*

## PROTECTION and FUSES

As explained in *Power (And All That Gubbins)*, amplifiers don't deeply appreciate being asked to drive ultra-low impedances or out-and-out short-circuits, and if it weren't for the use of protection circuits and/or fuses, they would show their displeasure fairly expensively.

Protection circuits come in two flavours: the self-resetting type, which waits maybe 30 seconds then tries to run the amp again, and the type where you actually have to turn the amp off and then on again. Either type might seem like a big improvement over having to grope around playing with fuses, but in practice, not all protection circuits are quite what they seem. Some are what might be called 'over-protective', and scream for help long before they really need to – since, at the very least, it means you lose power for 30 seconds or more every now and then, and, even when the amp is working, the protector often prevents you using its theoretical power capability to the full. This is a design 'feature' I don't find too endearing.

The dear old fuse may be a pest to replace, especially since you need to carry loads of them, just in case your first, second, or even 20th attempt at fixing the prob doesn't work, but at least they're unlikely to mess you around too often. Many amps use both protectors and fuses, but as far as fuses are concerned, the main thing is to look for an amp where the fuseholders are on the front panel – this makes replacement far easier than having to grope round the back.

## FANS

Not the sort who pay to sweat at your gigs, but the kind you pay to stop your amp(s) sweating. Some operate whenever the power is on, others only kick in when the temperature inside the amp rises – either way, the really important point is that fans will only do what they're supposed to do if you leave at least an inch or two of space around both inlet and outlet vents.

## ACTIVE CROSSOVERS and BI-/TRI-AMPING

OK, so an active crossover isn't, in itself, a power amplifier, but as we'll see in the *Speakers* chapter, though normal crossovers may be cheap, they're a very inefficient way of doing the job. Active crossovers perform the same task of dividing the frequency spectrum into the appropriate parts for each drive unit, but don't absorb/waste any of your power, because they're really nothing more than specially-designed EQ controls.

Unfortunately, active crossovers don't come cheap, not because they're particularly complicated, but simply because the market for them is relatively small – which isn't surprising, given you can only sensibly use them when you've got to the stage of running enough total power to justify having several power amps (one for each part of the spectrum).

As you might guess, bi-amping is for two-way speakers, tri- for three-ways: you can get both types of active crossover, but there's something to be said for one that can support both modes of operation, so you don't have to dump it if/when you move up from bi- to tri-amping.

# SELECTED
# POWER AMPLIFIERS

## EXAMPLES OF CURRENT MODELS

(This list is NOT intended to be comprehensive,
or to recommend some models above others)

### PEAVEY CS200X – 1U rackmount – £389

◆ 2 x 85 watts into 4 ohms; 220 watts into 4 ohms bridged mono
◆ Calibrated, detented level controls
◆ Built-in compression with LED indicator
◆ Jack input connectors
◆ Rear panel bridge and ground-lift switches
◆ Binding post and jack speaker outputs

### CROWN 460CSL – 2U rackmount – £499

◆ 2 x 230 watts into 4 ohms; 430 watts into 8 ohms bridged mono
◆ Grounded bridge output
◆ ODEP protection circuitry
◆ Good protection against DC permits high current/voltage operation
◆ Three year warranty

### YAMAHA P1500 – 3U rackmount – £499

◆ 2 x 150 watts into 8 ohms; 420 watts into 8 ohms bridged mono
◆ Protection, signal, clip and power LEDs
◆ 41-click rotary input attenuators

*Carlsbro's CPX family includes the CPX800 (second from bottom) which,*
*for £579, delivers 2 x 400 watts into 4 ohms (see next page)*

✦ Recessed power switch
✦ Comprehensive protection circuitry
✦ Jack, XLR and barrier strip input connectors
✦ Two-speed, low-noise cooling fan
✦ Rear panel stereo/bridged mono switch

## CARLSBRO CPX800 – 3U rackmount – £579

◆ 2 x 400 watts into 4 ohms; 1170 watts into 4 ohms bridged mono
◆ Balanced inputs on XLR and jack connectors
◆ Short circuit, DC, and sub audio protection circuitry
◆ Two-speed fan cooling
◆ Soft start power supply with audio muting
◆ Neutrik Speakon and binding post speaker outputs

## CREST AUDIO Vs450 – 3U rackmount – £581

◆ 2 x 225 watts into 4 ohms; 450 watts into 8 ohms bridged mono
◆ Frequency response 10Hz-65kHz
◆ Signal, clip, protect and active clip LEDs
◆ Large extruded heatsink and four-inch fan
◆ Rear-panel volume controls
◆ Crest Tourclass Protection includes Active Clip Limiting preventing distortion and damage
◆ Slightly dearer V series has 20-segment meters and front panel volume controls

## STUDIOMASTER 700D – 2U rackmount – £583

◆ 2 x 350 watts into 4 ohms; 700 watts into 8 ohms bridged mono
◆ Signal, clip, power, bridge and mono LEDs
◆ Calibrated level controls
◆ Delayed power-on protection
◆ AMCS protection circuitry
◆ Balanced XLR and jack input connectors
◆ Variable speed cooling fan
◆ Rear panel bridge and mono switches
◆ Ground-lift switch

## YAMAHA P2500 – 3U rackmount – £599

◆ 2 x 250 watts into 8 ohms; 700 watts into 8 ohms bridged mono
◆ Protection, signal, clip and power LEDs
◆ 41-click rotary input attenuators
◆ Recessed power switch
◆ Comprehensive protection circuitry
◆ Jack, XLR and barrier strip input connectors
◆ Two-speed, low-noise cooling fan
◆ Rear panel stereo/bridged mono switch

## QSC USA 850 – 3U rackmount – £646

◆ 2 x 425 watts into 8 ohms; 800 watts into 4 ohms bridged mono
◆ Clip and power LEDs
◆ Comprehensive protection circuitry
◆ Balanced or unbalanced jack input connectors
◆ Two-speed cooling fan
◆ Rear panel bridged mono switch

*QSC USA 850: 2 x 425 watts into 8 ohms or 800 watts into 4 ohms mono*

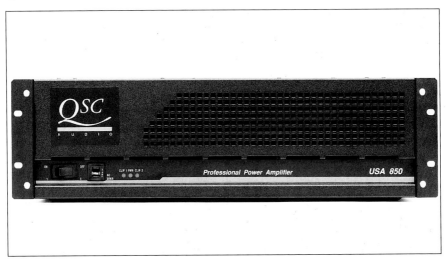

*Opposite, top: Peavey CS1000X delivers 2 x 525 watts into 4 ohms;
bottom: Crown 1400CSL has a 2 x 700 watt rating (see next page)*

## STUDIOMASTER 1200D – 2U rackmount – £763

✦ 2 x 600 watts into 4 ohms; 1200 watts into 8 ohms bridged mono
✦ Signal, clip, power, bridge and mono LEDs
✦ Calibrated level controls
✦ Delayed power-on protection
✦ AMCS protection circuitry
✦ Balanced XLR and jack input connectors
✦ Variable speed cooling fan
✦ Rear panel bridge, mono, and ground-lift switches
✦ Neutrik Speakon outputs

## H/H MX500 – 2U rackmount – £749

✦ 2 x 250 watts into 4 ohms; 500 watts into 8 ohms bridged mono
✦ Signal, peak, protection and limiter LEDs
✦ Switchable active clip limiting
✦ Comprehensive protection
✦ Balanced XLR and jack input connectors
✦ Variable speed cooling fan
✦ Rear panel bridge and mono switches
✦ Ground-lift switch
✦ Neutrik Speakon and binding post outputs

## PEAVEY CS1000X – 3U rackmount – £799

✦ 2 x 525 watts into 4 ohms; 1500 watts into 4 ohms bridged mono
✦ Bargraph signal level indicators
✦ Protection LEDs
✦ Calibrated level controls
✦ Built-in compression with LED indicators and defeat switch
✦ Balanced XLR and jack input connectors
✦ Auto two-speed speed cooling fan
✦ Rear panel bridge switch
✦ Binding post and jack speaker outputs

## CREST AUDIO Vs1100 – 3U rackmount – £922

◆ 2 x 550 watts into 4 ohms; 1100 watts into 8 ohms bridged mono
◆ Frequency response 10Hz-65kHz
◆ Signal, clip, protect and active clip LEDs
◆ Large extruded heatsink and four-inch fan
◆ Rear-panel volume controls
◆ Tourclass Protection includes ACL, preventing speaker damage
◆ Also 'V' series with 20-segment meters and front panel controls

## CROWN 1400CSL – 2U RACKMOUNT – £939

✦ 2 x 700 watts into 4 ohms; 1000 watts into 8 ohms bridged mono
✦ Grounded bridge output
✦ ODEP protection circuitry
✦ Good protection against DC permits high current/voltage operation
✦ Three-year warranty

## QSC USA 1300 – 4U RACKMOUNT – £975

✦ 2 x 650 watts into 8 ohms; 1300 watts into 4 ohms bridged mono
✦ Clip and power LEDs
✦ Comprehensive protection circuitry
✦ Balanced or unbalanced jack input connectors
✦ Two-speed cooling fan
✦ Rear panel bridged mono switch

## C-AUDIO RA1001 – 2U RACKMOUNT – £1048

✦ 2 x 250 watts into 4 ohms; 500 watts into 8 ohms bridged mono
✦ Electronically balanced inputs on XLR and jack connectors
✦ Neutrik Speakon output connectors
✦ Built-in amplifier and speaker protection
✦ Ground-lift switch

## H/H MX1200 – 2U RACKMOUNT – £1099

✦ 2 x 600 watts into 4 ohms; 900 watts into 8 ohms bridged mono
✦ Signal, peak, protection and limiter LEDs
✦ Switchable active clip limiting
✦ Comprehensive protection
✦ Balanced XLR and jack input connectors
✦ Variable speed cooling fan
✦ Rear panel bridge and mono switches
✦ Ground-lift switch
✦ Neutrik Speakon and binding post outputs

# MIXER-AMPS/ POWERED MIXERS

The idea of combining a mixer and a power amp in one box makes sense for much the same reasons as combining the pre-amp and power amp in backline kit – ie there's only one box, so it cuts manufacturing and shipping costs. It also means you need fewer cables, and only one power supply – and it (hopefully) means the two elements are well-matched to work together.

But... there can be drawbacks; the most obvious being that if, for example, the mixer section breaks down and has to go for service, you lose your power amp as well. Also, if you want a high-power unit, you'll quite possibly end up paying for mixer features you might not need; or, conversely, if you want a highly-spec'd mixer, you might be paying for power you don't currently need.

This happens simply because the designers of these beasties tend to put together what they regard as 'balanced' products, where more features go hand-in-hand with more power. Most of the time they're right, but it's a bit like buying a ready-made suit: if it fits, fine, you're saving a good few bucks – but you might just be a non-standard size/have non-standard needs.

Still, that cost-saving aspect is particularly relevant at the budget end of the market, and it's here competition is fiercest – which is good in one way, because it gives you the maximum choice. The other side of the coin is, having all that choice, you really need to spend quite some time sifting through the umpteen options in order to make your best buying decision.

Most budget mixer-amps tend to follow a well-established formula: you'll typically have six input channels, each with two-band EQ, one or maybe two effect sends (one for reverb/echo, one for foldback – remember you'll need an outboard power amp or powered monitor speakers to use this), and a master section with an effect return, master level, plus some sort of graphic EQ.

This type of EQ (generally five or seven-band) is often fine for matching speakers to your preferred sound, and even for compensating

*Dynamix Powermix 16/2 incorporates two ART digital FX processors*

for venue acoustics, but, as we'll see in *Soundchecks*, pretty much irrelevant when it comes to fixing feedback problems. The power amp will be mono, which is not a problem, since these amps are most-commonly used only for vocals, and the power will be in the 150-250 watt range.

Feature-wise, as mentioned in *Mixers*, I'd say if you're going to use foldback, then a switch/level control to bring the effect return into the foldback mix is a Very Good Thing – as is a low-cut/bass roll-off filter on each channel, though few basic mixer-amps sport this cheap but incredibly useful item.

Mixer-amps are traditionally laid out like backline amp heads, with their controls on the front, rather than the conventional controls-on-top mixer lay-out, but this usually works perfectly well in most cases, as it's rather unlikely you'd be trying to do hands-on mixing in the kind of applications these mixers are generally used for (ie small venues where there's no sound engineer). The main thing is to find somewhere (on top of the backline?) to place the kit, where it's raised up enough for you to get at it easily if you do need to make mid-gig changes.

Once you move up from the cheapest of the budget stuff, the number of channels, the features on each channel, and the power all tend to increase. You're also likely to start finding inserts on the channels and/or the master section, the latter being especially useful if you want to patch a compressor/limiter and/or a serious graphic EQ into the system, both of which can make a lot of sense for delivering your music more effectively (see *Effects*).

By the time you get to £800-£1000 mixer-amps, you're into the kind of territory where you can reasonably start thinking about buying a separate mixer and power amp, which gives you the freedom to build the system the way you want it. Interestingly, this is around the start of the price-bracket where we've recently seen an explosive growth in 'powered mixers'. Here the mixer is laid out like a recording-style desk, the built-in power amp is stereo (fine even if you'll be running it in mono), and, on the more expensive units, basic reverb/echo effects are on-board.

I can well understand the attraction of these products, because they save you making a whole pile of mix & match decisions, but there's still the fundamental point that, if one part of the product decides to die, you're without the whole lot while it's being serviced, which is not something I find too appealing. There are some fine products being sold in this area, but it's safest to make an on-loan replacement deal with your retailer before you buy such an item – and maybe carry a cheap mixer amp to gigs as an emergency back-up...

# SELECTED MIXER-AMPS / POWERED MIXERS

## EXAMPLES OF CURRENT MODELS

(This list is NOT intended to be comprehensive,
or to recommend some models above others)

### TORQUE T150PA – £295

✦ 4/1 mixer-amp
✦ 150 watts power amplifier
✦ Four high/low impedance input channels, each with two-band EQ
✦ Presence and reverb depth controls
✦ Signal routing switch with LED indicator
✦ Effects send and return, footswitch, auxiliary and slave output jacks
✦ Twin speaker output jacks

### LANEY TH150X5 – £319

✦ 5/1 mixer-amp
✦ 150 watts power amplifier
✦ Five input channels, each with two-band EQ
✦ Balanced XLR mike inputs, jack line inputs (ch 1 has jack & phono)
✦ Effects loop send and return
✦ Built-in reverb

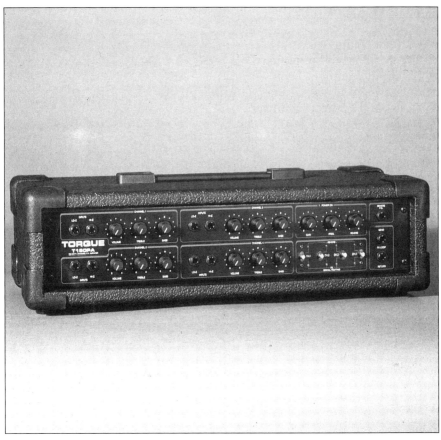

*Torque T150PA: entry-level 4-channel 150 watt mixer amp for just £295*

## PEAVEY XR500C – £399

- ✦ 5/1 mixer-amp
- ✦ 150 watts power amplifier
- ✦ Five input channels, each with two-band EQ
- ✦ Balanced XLR mike inputs, jack line inputs
- ✦ Post effects send
- ✦ Seven-band graphic equaliser
- ✦ DDT compression
- ✦ Monitor gain, reverb return, patch panel (interface with aux devices)

## FENDER SR-6300P – £510

+ 6/1 mixer-amp
+ 300 watts power amplifier
+ Six input channels, each with two-band EQ
+ Balanced XLR mike inputs, jack line inputs
+ Nine-band graphic equaliser
+ DeltaComp compression circuitry
+ Independent stage monitor mix

## CARLSBRO GRX7 – £529

+ 6/1 mixer-amp
+ 400 watts power amplifier
+ Six input channels, each with three-band EQ
+ Balanced XLR mike inputs, jack line inputs
+ Effects send and return
+ Nine-band graphic equaliser
+ Accutronics spring reverb

## TORQUE T730PA – £600

+ 7/1 mixer-amp
+ 300 watts power amplifier
+ Six input channels, each with three-band EQ
+ Balanced XLR mike inputs, jack line inputs
+ Phono tape input with three-band EQ
+ Effects send and return
+ Nine-band graphic equaliser
+ Accutronics spring reverb

*Peaey XRD 680S includes digital stereo effects with 120-plus presets*

## PEAVEY XRD680S – £629

✦ 8/2 mixer-amp
✦ 2x150 watts power amplifiers
✦ Eight input channels, each with three-band active EQ
✦ High & low impedance, balanced inputs on each channel
✦ Digital stereo effects (over 120 presets)
✦ Nine-band graphic EQ (& patch for external graphic)
✦ DDT compression
✦ Pre-monitor send
✦ Stereo tape outs and ins
✦ Selectable phantom power

## STUDIOMASTER POWERHOUSE VISION 8 – £1174

✦ 8/2 powered mixer
✦ 350 watts per channel power amplifier
✦ Built-in digital FX unit (127 effects, inc reverb, delay, echo...)
✦ XLR and jack mike/line inputs
✦ Trim controls, three-band EQ, three auxiliaries, and pan controls
✦ Stereo aux return
✦ Tape record/playback phono socket
✦ Two independent assignable seven-band graphic equalisers
✦ Fully protected against short circuit overload

## H/H MISCARA M1002PD – £1099

✦ 10/2 mixer-amp
✦ 300 watts per channel power amplifier
✦ Built-in 127 program digital multi-effects unit
✦ Ten inputs: six mono mike or line, two stereo
✦ Three-band EQ on all inputs
✦ Pad switch and phantom power on mike channels
✦ Pad switch and graphic EQ switch on all inputs
✦ Eight-band graphic equaliser with balance control
✦ Subsonic filter with 18dB/octave roll-off below 100Hz
✦ Stereo tape input
✦ Ten-LED bargraph meter

## DYNAMIX POWERMIX 16/2 – £1249

✦ 16/2 powered mixer
✦ 600 watts per channel power amplifier
✦ Two on-board ART digital effects processors (32 reverbs and effects)
✦ 12 mike or line inputs, plus four independent stereo ins, with level
✦ Inserts on all channels
✦ Phantom power on selected channels
✦ Three-band EQ, including mid sweep
✦ Four aux sends per channel
✦ On-board active crossover
✦ Ten-LED bargraph meter

*Spirit Powerstation offers a built-in Lexicon digital multi-effects unit*

## SPIRIT POWERSTATION – £1367

✦ 12/2 powered mixer
✦ 300 watts per channel power amplifier
✦ Built-in Lexicon digital multi-effects unit
✦ Freestanding or rackmountable
✦ 12 inputs: eight mono, two stereo
✦ Stereo seven-band graphic equaliser with bypass switch
✦ Subsonic filter with 18dB/octave roll-off below 100Hz
✦ Three-band EQ on all inputs
✦ Dedicated two-track send and return
✦ Ten-LED bargraph meter

*Studiomaster Powerhouse Horizon is a top spec powered mixer with 16 inputs, 2 x 600 watts output and programmable stereo digital effects*

## STUDIOMASTER POWERHOUSE HORIZON – £1761

◆ 12/2 powered mixer – 16 inputs total: eight mike (jack or XLR), three stereo line, & stereo tape
◆ 600 watts per channel power amplifier
◆ Programmable stereo digital effects with MIDI and alphanumeric display
◆ 2 x seven-band assignable graphic EQ
◆ Three-band EQ with mid sweep on each channel
◆ Four auxiliary sends
◆ LED metering
◆ Steel construction; optional rack-mount kit

## FENDER PX2216D – £1890

◆ 16/2 mixer and amp combination
◆ 300 watts per channel power amplifier
◆ Built-in digital multi-effects unit
◆ Case houses mixer and amp and doubles as stand
◆ 16 mike or line inputs, with insert points on all
◆ Three-band EQ on all inputs
◆ Two nine-band graphic equalisers
◆ Two monitor mixes
◆ Bargraph meters for outputs

# SPEAKERS

In *Backline* I avoid going into the precise details of how a loudspeaker works, and I'm not going to do it here either, as it's not terribly important the user should know – suffice to say whatever you feed into your power amp(s) should come out here. There are, however, some vital elements you should be familiar with.

## IMPEDANCE

This is fundamentally important stuff – if you haven't already read the Power (And Some Other Tech Talk) chapter, now might be a Good Time, because this is very definitely an instance where ignorance is far from bliss, and not knowing at least the basics can have annoying (and expensive) results.

## TWO-WAY SPEAKERS

Almost certainly the type of compact PA speakers you'll be buying. They're called two-way because there are two drive units (individual speakers) in a single cabinet, much as in many hi-fi set-ups – one handling bass and mid frequencies, and the other taking care of the top end. The bigger the bass/mid speaker, generally speaking, the better the reproduction of the bass end – I say generally, because, as you'll see in *Backline*, several small units can be more effective than one big one. In the case of most semi-pro kit, though, you'll usually find a 12 or 15 inch driver.

The top end will almost certainly be 'horn'-loaded (see Cabinet Types below), and the bottom end ported (or 'reflex'-loaded – usually identifiable by a slot or space at the bottom of the cab), to help the bass/mid driver deliver maximum bass for minimum amp power. Inside the cab there will be a basic passive crossover (see Crossovers below), and, possibly, a considerable amount of acoustic wadding to damp unwanted resonances.

If you're just aiming to stick vocals through the PA, then you can get away with a speaker of fairly small size – 12in bass/mid and a horn tweeter – though a lot of vocalists like the warmer tonal quality that a 15in bass driver typically provides. If you intend to mike up instruments in the future, it could be worth investing in the bigger beastie right from the start, because 15-inchers are more likely to handle powerful bass effectively.

## THREE-WAY SPEAKERS

Similarly designed to the two-way variety, the three-way incorporates an additional driver, which handles the mid frequencies, and a more complex crossover system.

Both two-way and three-way speakers are designed to be used with the top-end at the top (yes, people do use them the wrong way round), and you'll generally need to get them up high in pub and club environments, to stop the punters soaking up too much of your mid and top end sound (see below, and in *Creating Your Sound*).

## SUBWOOFER and SATELLITE SYSTEMS

Totally separating the low frequencies from the mid and top end by using a subwoofer plus satellite speakers is the way top-line dance clubs achieve their sound, and it can also work well for live music – most big concerts use this method. But, for pub/club gigging, it's probably not the best way to go, mainly because it involves bi- or tri-amping and active crossovers, and these mean mucho mazuma. It certainly enables the top end to shine through more efficiently, and can give gut-thumping power to the bass – but unless you spend really big bucks on the system, you'd probably be paying more for image than actual sound quality.

## COMPONENT SYSTEMS

When you move up in the market (and spend a deal more dosh), you get into the realms of 'designer' PA: component speaker systems tailored to operate with bi- or tri-amping to maximum effect. These systems usually feature cabinets that are trapezoidal in shape (big front, small back, sides taper) for mounting in 'clusters' above the stage (known as 'flying'), and they'll be designed to use active crossovers (see below). A

*Celestion's good-looking new Road Series – see page 98 for sample specs*

great advantage with these systems is that you can expand them by adding more, and maybe bigger, units as your popularity and pocket dictate (or, looking on the sad side, flogging a few when you're no longer flavour of the month).

## CROSSOVERS

The basic reason for using a crossover (filter) is that big bass/mid drivers don't do a good job of producing top end, and treble units have a tendency to fly half-way across the room if you ask them to handle bass.

In most basic two-way PA speakers the crossovers are very simple items, but, no matter how simple, they do waste amplifier power, which is why the big-time guys and gals prefer to use active systems. Active (independently powered) crossovers are basically fixed-EQ controls stuck before the amps (see *Power Amplifiers*). Once again, there's nothing very sophisticated about them – they just do the job a lot more efficiently, by sending the appropriate frequencies to the appropriate drive unit's power amp.

## CABINET TYPES –
## INFINITE BAFFLE (SEALED BOX), REFLEX and HORN

Sealed box speakers provide, in many respects, the ideal way to produce extended and well-defined bass – but their drawbacks are that the cabs need to be quite large, and they're not noted for high sensitivity at the bass end.

Reflex loading uses a small vent/port/gap in the enclosure to tune/enhance the speaker's resonance, so deep bass output is improved in quantity (thereby effectively making the speaker more sensitive), though, in most cases, at the expense of a small loss of definition/tightness. Reflex loading is the most commonly used system for PA speakers.

A horn, which can be a variety of shapes and sizes, is basically a way of projecting a speaker's sound more effectively – based on the principle of old the old gramophone horn. The term is most commonly used in connection with treble speakers. Horns for bass use (also known as bins, mainly because they look like rubbish skips) need to be very, very large (sell the Transit, and start looking for a second-hand removal van), but, in many ways, they're the ideal way of doing the job, because they can provide incredibly high sensitivity, and, usually, without losing out in the definition stakes.

*Part of Trace-Elliot's Evolution Series – see page 101 for details*

Over the past ten years or so, there's been a major trend towards making PA speakers as small as possible – this makes obvious sense from the point of view of getting the little darlings into the back of your Mini Metro, and small speakers can deliver fine results on vocals in the typical pub environment. But, if you're going to be running instruments through your PA, and/or playing larger venues, then I seriously urge you to consider some much larger speakers, even if you can only find them at sensible prices on the second-hand market – these are much more likely to deliver a 'big' sound, and horn-loaded ones can be particularly brill.

(A short story: a local band had a pair of utterly superb, but utterly enormous horn beasts – six foot by three by three, they weighed well over a hundredweight each, and would have made excellent coffins, for which purpose they might well have been needed, had they ever fallen on anyone. Not surprisingly, the band got fed up lugging them in and out of pubs, so they sold them and bought a mini pair. Great, they said, we should have done this years ago. Trouble was, the new speakers were bloody awful, and punters started coming up to them and asking why the band suddenly sounded so crappy. Quick rethink, followed by increasingly begging phone calls to purchaser of old speakers, who finally sold them back to the band for twice what he'd paid for them...)

## TRIPOD MOUNTING

Underneath most small and mid-size speaker cabs you should find a hole, known as a top-hat (because it looks like a very small one when it's not in the speaker), which accepts the end of a speaker stand's mounting pole. It's worth investing in really sturdy (ie expensive) stands – I personally have deep reservations about the use of cheap stands for speakers, unless they're kept well away from both musicians and punters. Please don't even think about mounting your speakers on stands primarily intended for use with dainty things like mikes, or trying to balance them precariously on beer crates, tables and the like. And make sure you gaffer-tape the cables down. Speakers are heavy, musicians can be clumsy, and punters may be both fragile and have litigiously-inclined lawyers.

## CONNECTORS

In the beginning there were binding posts (for attaching bare speaker wires), and you'll still find them on some speakers, but most now have jacks and/or XLRs, while many up-market models sport Speakon connectors (see *Power Amplifiers*). Most PA speakers have an output as well as an input, so you can connect one speaker to another – as a general rule, don't plug in more than one extra speaker, or you could end up with the impedance being so low as to push your amp towards Expensive Repair Syndrome (see Impedance back in *Power (And Some Other Tech Talk)*). Whatever type of connectors your speakers have, don't use them with cables intended for mike or line work – you'll lose bass response.

# SELECTED SPEAKERS

## EXAMPLES OF CURRENT MODELS

(This list is NOT intended to be comprehensive,
or to recommend some models above others)


### LANEY TE100 – TWO-WAY SPEAKER – £216 PER PAIR

- ✦ 10in mid/bass driver and bullet tweeter
- ✦ Power-handling: 120 watts per pair
- ✦ Impedance: 8 ohms
- ✦ Size: 460mm (H) 350mm (W) 265mm (D)
- ✦ Finish: Black


### PEAVEY EUROSYS 1 – TWO-WAY SPEAKER – £249 PER PAIR

- ✦ 10in mid/bass driver and tweeter
- ✦ Power-handling: 130 watts per pair
- ✦ Impedance: 8 ohms
- ✦ Sensitivity: 95dB at 1 metre for 1 watt
- ✦ Size: 525mm (H) 370mm (W) 280mm (D)
- ✦ Finish: Black carpet


### TORQUE TS100H – TWO-WAY SPEAKER – £260 PER PAIR

- ✦12in mid/bass driver and bullet tweeter
- ✦ Power-handling: 200 watts per pair
- ✦ Impedance: 8 ohms
- ✦ Size: 520mm (H) 430mm (W) 280mm (D)
- ✦ Finish: Black

## PEAVEY EUROSYS 2 – TWO-WAY SPEAKER – £289 PER PAIR

- ✦ 12in mid/bass driver and treble horn
- ✦ Power-handling: 200 watts per pair
- ✦ Impedance: 8 ohms
- ✦ Sensitivity: 95dB at 1 metre for 1 watt
- ✦ Size: 610mm (H) 420mm (W) 285mm (D)
- ✦ Finish: Black carpet

*Made in Europe –*
*Fender's ELC*
*Series speakers*

## FENDER ELC-112 – TWO-WAY SPEAKER – £332 PER PAIR

- ✦ 12in mid/bass driver and treble horn
- ✦ Power-handling: 300 watts per pair
- ✦ Impedance: 8 ohms
- ✦ Sensitivity: 97dB at 1 metre for 1 watt
- ✦ Size: 565mm (H) 457mm (W) 375mm (D)
- ✦ Finish: Black carpet

## FENDER ELC-115 – TWO-WAY SPEAKER – £376 PER PAIR

◆ 15in mid/bass driver and treble horn
◆ Power-handling: 300 watts per pair
◆ Impedance: 8 ohms
◆ Sensitivity: 98dB at 1 metre for 1 watt
◆ Size: 648mm (H) 520mm (W) 425mm (D)
◆ Finish: Black carpet

## LANEY TE300 – TWO-WAY SPEAKER – £360 PER PAIR

◆ 15in mid/bass driver and treble horn
◆ Power-handling: 300 watts per pair
◆ Impedance: 8 ohms
◆ Size: 640mm (H) 490mm (W) 355mm (D)
◆ Finish: Black

## TORQUE TS215H – TWO-WAY SPEAKER – £390 PER PAIR

◆ 15in mid/bass driver and two bullet tweeters
◆ Power-handling: 400 watts per pair
◆ Impedance: 8 ohms
◆ Size: 600mm (H) 510mm (W) 320mm (D)
◆ Finish: Black

## CARLSBRO BETA 112 – TWO-WAY SPEAKER – £532 PER PAIR

◆ 12in mid/bass driver and treble horn
◆ Power-handling: 300 watts each
◆ Impedance: 4 or 8 ohms
◆ Sensitivity: 96dB at 1 metre for 1 watt
◆ Size: 520mm (H) 380mm (W) 270mm (D)
◆ Finish: Black

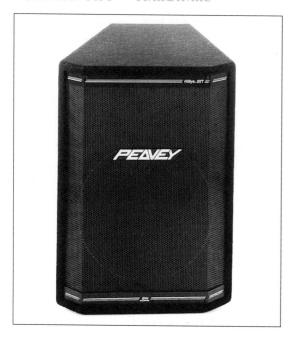

*Left: Peavey's UK-made Hisys 2XT 15in mid/bass driver handles 350 watts RMS*

## CARLSBRO BETA 115 – two-way speaker – £599 per pair

◆ 15in mid/bass driver and treble horn
◆ Power-handling: 300 watts each
◆ Impedance: 4 or 8 ohms
◆ Sensitivity: 98dB at 1 metre for 1 watt
◆ Size: 670mm (H) 490mm (W) 330mm (D)
◆ Finish: Black

## PEAVEY HISYS 2XT – two-way speaker – £698 per pair

◆ 15in low frequency driver and treble horn
◆ Power-handling: 350 watts RMS each
◆ Impedance: 4 or 8 ohms
◆ Sensitivity: 98 dB at 1 metre for 1 watt
◆ Size: 690mm (H) 500mm (W) 375mm (D)
◆ Passive crossover design
◆ Finish: Black carpet

*Fostex SPA11: two 4in full-range drivers powered by integral 100W amp*

## PEAVEY IMPULSE 200 – two-way speaker – £699 per pair (pre-release info)

- ✦ 12in mid/bass driver and treble horn
- ✦ Power-handling: 300 watts each
- ✦ Sensitivity: 101 dB at 1 metre for 1 watt
- ✦ Finish: Black/moulded cabs

## FOSTEX SPA11 – powered PA speaker for solo acts/duos – £724 per pair

- ✦ Two 4in full-range drivers in bass reflex enclosure
- ✦ 100 watts RMS power amplifier
- ✦ Mike and line inputs plus aux output on jack sockets
- ✦ Sensitivity: 98dB at 1 metre for 1 watt
- ✦ Size: 180mm (H) 350mm (W) 211mm (D)
- ✦ Finish: Black polyester/fibre plastic

## CELESTION ROAD 1220 – two-way speaker – £730 per pair

✦ 12in mid/bass driver and treble horn
✦ Power-handling: 250 watts each
✦ Impedance: 8 ohms
✦ Sensitivity: 97dB at 1 metre for 1 watt
✦ Size: 640mm (H) 373mm (W) 333mm (D)
✦ Jack and Speakon connectors
✦ Finish: Dark Grey

## JBL TR125 – two-way speaker – £749 per pair

✦ 15in mid/bass driver and treble horn
✦ Power handling: 225 watts each
✦ Impedance: 8 ohms
✦ Sensitivity: 99dB at 1 metre for 1 watt
✦ Size: 750mm (H) 460mm (W) 370 (D)
✦ Built-in SonicGuard Protection circuitry

## TURBOSOUND IMPACT 80 – two-way speaker – £822 per pair

✦ 8in mid/bass driver and treble horn
✦ Power-handling: 125 watts each
✦ Impedance: 16 ohms
✦ Sensitivity: 91 dB at 1 metre for 1 watt
✦ Size: 440mm (H) 295mm (W) 238mm (D)
✦ Finish: Grey or TurboBlue

## CELESTION ROAD 1520 – two-way speaker – £998 per pair

✦ 15in mid/bass driver and treble horn
✦ Power-handling: 300 watts each
✦ Impedance: 8 ohm
✦ Sensitivity: 99dB at 1 metre for 1 watt
✦ Size: 745mm (H) 475mm (W) 445mm (D)
✦ Jack and Speakon connectors
✦ Finish: Dark Grey

*Martin Audio ICT300: two 10in drivers handle an impressive 300 watts*

## RAMSA A200 – two-way speAker – £1093 per pAir

♦ 12in mid/bass driver and treble horn
♦ Power-handling: 125 watts RMS each
♦ Impedance: 8 ohms
♦ Sensitivity: 98dB at 1 metre for 1 watt
♦ Size: 577mm (H) 395mm (W) 273mm (D)
♦ Finish: Black

## MARTIN AUDIO ICT 300 two-way speAker – £1163 per pAir

♦ Twin 10in drivers, horizontally mounted (Inductively Coupled)
♦ Power handling: 300 watts each
♦ Impedance: 8 ohms
♦ Sensitivity: 96dB at 1 metre for 1 watt
♦ Size: 325mm (H) 565mm (W) 325mm (D)
♦ Finish: Textured black paint

*Turbosound Impact 80, 120 and 180 feature 8in, 12in and 18in drivers*

### TURBOSOUND IMPACT 120 – TWO-WAY SPEAKER – £1204 PER PAIR

✦ 12in mid/bass driver and treble horn
✦ Power-handling: 200 watts each
✦ Impedance: 8 ohms
✦ Sensitivity: 94dB at 1 metre for 1 watt
✦ Size: 703mm (H) 390mm (W) 356mm (D)
✦ Finish: Grey or TurboBlue


### ELECTROVOICE SX200 – TWO-WAY SPEAKER – £1384 PER PAIR

✦ 12in mid/bass driver with compression driver
✦ Impedance: 8 ohms
✦ Power handling: 300 watts each
✦ Sensitivity: 101.5 dB at 1 metre for 1 watt
✦ Size: 587mm (H) 429mm (W) 312mm (D)
✦ Finish: Black

## JBL M330 Mk2 – two-way speaker – £1407 per pair

◆ 12in mid/bass driver and treble horn
◆ Power handling: 350 watts each
◆ Impedance: 8 ohms
◆ Sensitivity: 99dB at 1 metre for 1 watt
◆ Size: 700mm (H) 460mm (W) 390mm (D)
◆ Finish: Black

## RCF EVENT 1000 – two-way speaker – £1539 per pair

◆ 12in mid/bass driver; 1in HF compression driver in constant directivity horn
◆ Impedance: 8 ohms
◆ Power handling: 300 watts RMS each
◆ Sensitivity: 101 dB at 1 metre for 1 watt
◆ Size: 800mm (H) 565mm (W) 410mm (D)
◆ Finish: Black

## TRACE ELLIOT EVOLUTION 1 – three-way speaker – £1598 per pair

◆ 15in bass driver, 10in mid-range unit and horn HF driver
◆ Impedance: 8 ohms
◆ Power handling: 350 watts each
◆ Sensitivity: 96 dB at 1 metre for 1 watt
◆ Size: 445mm (H) 605mm (W) 610mm (D)
◆ Finish: Black

## BOSE 802 SERIES 2 – popular with (well-paid) solos/duos – £1756 per pair

◆ Eight full-range drivers
◆ Power handling: up to 240 watts RMS each
◆ Impedance: 8 ohms
◆ Sensitivity: 91dB at 1 metre for 1 watt
◆ Size: 340mm (H) 520mm (W) 330mm (D)
◆ Finish: black polyethylene

BRITAIN'S SKINNIEST MUSICIANS' MAGAZINE
FEBRUARY 1996 ♦ ISSUE 119

# MAKING MUSIC

**Win**
A Roland XP-IO Synth
A Korg AX3OG FX

# Skunk Anansie

**Node**
**Leonard Cohen**
**MU vs IMF**

Reviews: ● Korg Trinity ● Gus GI Guitar ● Marshall JTM6IO ● Pearl Snare/Pedals

● Choosing Venues
● Tony Visconti
● Dave Lombardo

**Wildhearts**
**Echobelly**

**PJ Harvey**
**Dub War** ●
**Black Sabbath** ●
**Arranging Songs** ●

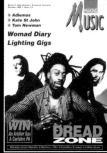

● Adiemus
● Kate St John
● Tom Newman

**Womad Diary**
**Lighting Gigs**

**WIN**
An Arbiter Sax
A Carlsbro PA

**DREAD ZONE**

# MAKING MUSIC

*Making Music* is Britain's most popular musicians' magazine (180,000 readers a month).

Whether you use a guitar, a sequencer, a drumkit or just your own voice, if you're into creating, recording or performing music, we've got something for you.

We're the only magazine that covers the whole music-making experience - from banging out tunes in your bedroom, to polishing your act, giving up the day job, signing deals, coping with fame (if that's what you want)...

Our interviews reveal how well-known artists work - how the records you buy and the gigs you see are put together: Skunk Anansie making their live sound fit the studio... Polly Harvey on song-writing and using your voice... Dreadzone discussing sampling and the beauty of dub...

Our features have lots of practical help on doing it yourself: which gear does what; how to build an audience; which record companies might be interested; and why it's not the end of the

world if they're not...

Get *Making Music* every month - pick it up in musical instrument shops or Virgin Megastores.

(Or subscribe for just £18 a year by ringing 01858 435 344.)

*Making Music*, Nexus House, Swanley, Kent BR8 8HY. Tel: 01322 660070
Fax: 01322 615636

# EFFECTS

Lots of musicians will already be familiar with lots of effects – the majority of which are probably in an ever-growing pedal pile on the floor in front of the guitarist. All effects add, or subtract, an electronic something to the original sound to change the result; we'll concern ourselves here with those that are useful for PA, and then mention a few popular models.

## LIMITERS

Not the most sophisticated of devices these, but almost universally used in pro PA, and definitely your first choice when spending your cash (very few are available as stand-alone units, most are combined with compressors – see below).

When you turn up the volume during a gig, you eventually reach a point where the amp stops producing pure volume, and just starts to add distortion, until it blows something expensive (like the amp) or something inconvenient (like a fuse). At the same time this kind of overload distortion is not very pleasing from the punter perspective – it could even put them off their beer. The promoter, landlord, or whoever, isn't going to like that.

Two solutions: spend big bucks on doubling the power of your PA, or spend two to three hundred quid on a limiter, which, by preventing signals from reaching critical levels, can make your PA sound like it's got twice the power. It also helps protect your speakers.

## COMPRESSORS

A compressor is a more useful version of a limiter. As its name suggests, it works by compressing or reducing the dynamic range, so quiet levels sound louder. It achieves this without actually increasing the peak level, but your overall sound comes out louder, so it's definitely a Good Thing, as louder almost always sounds better (as I've said before).

Compressors come in two flavours: soft knee (kicks in gently), and hard knee (kicks in hard), so it's a good idea to try both out before you buy and see which suits your style. As a rough guide, Jimi Hendrix would probably have chosen 'hard knee', and Hank Marvin 'soft knee'.

One very important feature is a threshold control, because you don't want nasty noise levels coming up with everything else; this gives you control by setting a level below which the compressor doesn't compress. Definitely best to choose a compressor with a threshold control.

About 99per cent of big pro bands use compressors, as well as limiters, on their PA systems, and that's possibly a good enough reason for you not to disagree.

## NOISE GATES and DYNAMIC NOISE LIMITERS

Noise gates are basically muting devices – they're called gates because they can either be open, which lets the signal through, or closed, which kills it; you set the threshold level at which the gate opens and closes.

You also have control over how quckly the gate opens (delay), and how fast it shuts (rate): you can have it slam shut in the middle of a dying note, or closing gently to allow the note a degree of decay (see *Working With Effects*). Noise gates are mainly used to avoid noise from channels that aren't contributing anything musically useful, and this tightens the sounds in the mix. Particularly useful for drum mikes (especially snare), as a gate will switch off the mike on any drum that isn't actually being hit.

Dynamic noise limiters are a more sophisticated version of noise gates, not simply opening or shutting the signal channel, but monitoring what's going on, and filtering out the treble when the signal is low, thereby reducing hiss. Can be useful in your mix, but aren't generally essential, if you haven't got the readies. They are, however, jolly useful at the end of effect pedal chains, which often add horrendous amounts of treble garbage.

## EQ

Shortest section in the book, as this is covered fully in *Mixers, Soundchecks* (Fighting Feedback), *Mixer Amps* and *Mixing Parts 1 & 2*.

*Yamaha's new Pro R3 digital reverb unit*

## ECHO and REVERB

I think we can take it as read that you know what echo is . Yell (or yodel, if you know no fear) into a canyon, and you hear the sound coming back at a lower volume as it's bounced off the canyon walls. Echo is very useful when doing gigs, as it can make even lousy singers sound halfway decent, by adding a depth that just isn't there on a flat signal.

Reverb is a totally different animal, even though it uses the same principles – it combines multiple echoes, so tightly time-packed together you don't hear them as separate echoes, but rather as a warm 'after-sound'. Some reverb units offer literally hundreds of different programs, others only a few. From a performance point of view, the main thing to consider is how easily you can access the programs you want.

As you'll see in *Soundchecks* and *Mixing,* your use of such effects will be at least partly dependent on the natural acoustics of the room or hall you're playing in.

## ENHANCERS

There are quite a few points here: the original enhancers simply extended the top end of the frequency spectrum, by creating new treble an octave higher than what was already there; more recent types often add some clever time and phase manipulation (we don't have space to go into details here) to give a 'lift' to whatever signal they're fed with, helping it 'drive' more effectively through the overall mix.

A more recent innovation is the bass enhancer, which adds new bass an octave lower than the existing bass, often with phase-shifting et cetera, which tightens the sound. This adds enormous power to the bass end, particularly where sub-woofer speakers are used; and, although it has been more of a top-line disco and studio product than a gigging one up to now, the bass enhancer has a major role to play in the future of live music, even in small venues.

A good bass enhancer will tighten your bass sounds as well as increasing their depth (but it does need careful setting, otherwise you could find your bass drive units ending up down the far end of the venue). As we'll see later there are products that achieve both bass and treble enhancement at a relatively reasonable cost.

Don't use treble enhancers on the overall mix – this just makes everything sound toppier, and the punters soon adjust to it, which kind of defeats the whole point. Treble enhancement should really only be applied to just one or two elements you want to stand out in the mix – the most common example being lead vocals.

## MULTI-EFFECT UNITS

These days, there's ever-more choice in multi-effect units, and ever-greater numbers of different effects stuffed into each box, to the point where you can have a virtually limitless variety in just one unit

It might seem like the answer to a dream to have a single 1U rack unit combining all the effects you're ever likely to need (probably plus a few hundred you won't), and being able to use them all at once. But (yes, there's always a 'but') remember that a single multi-effects unit, even though it may have stereo inputs and outputs, cannot usually be split to provide different effects on each of its two channels.

Another important point to consider is what order you can apply the effects in – it's nice to be able to choose whether you run your phaser before your flanger, or flanger before phaser (or whatever turns you on).

Bear in mind you'll need a true stereo (two channel) processor (for example, a compressor and/or reverb), if you want to use it on your live mix (unless, of course, you're using a mono system).

# SELECTED EFFECTS

## EXAMPLES OF CURRENT MODELS

(This list is not intended to be comprehensive,
or to recommend some models above others)

### DBX 163A – compressor/limiter – £186

✦ Single fader control and thumb-adjust level set
✦ Jack input and output on rear
✦ High impedance instrument input on front panel
✦ Use two side-by-side for master/slave stereo pair

### DRAWMER LX20 – dual expander/compressor – £229

✦ 'Soft knee' characteristic and variable attack and release times
✦ 40dB of gain
✦ LED bargraph meters
✦ Bypass switches
✦ Side chain insert points
✦ Stereo link switch
✦ Mute socket
✦ 1/4in jack inputs & outputs

### BEHRINGER AUTOCOM MDX 1200 – compressor/limiter/expander – £199

✦ Auto and manual compression modes – adjustable attack and release
✦ IRC (Interactive Ratio Control) – "super musical" expander/gate
✦ Dynamic Enhancer to keep music bright despite heavy compression
✦ Two external key inputs

## ALESIS 3630 COMPRESSOR – TWIN CHANNEL COMPRESSOR/LIMITER – £275

◆ Fully variable threshold
◆ Compression ratio, attack, release and output level controls
◆ Selectable peak/RMS
◆ Hard/soft knee compression styles
◆ Input/output metering
◆ Gain reduction metering
◆ Adjustable gate
◆ True stereo linkable operation


## DRAWMER DL241 – DUAL AUTO COMPRESSOR – £440

◆ Auto functions give optimum results with minimum set-up time
◆ Expander/gate with unique "Program Adaptive Expansion" circuitry
◆ Fast, smooth response eliminates threshold "chatter"
◆ Soft knee compressor
◆ Peak level limiting
◆ Bargraph metering


## DRAWMER DS201-XLR – FREQUENCY CONSCIOUS DUAL NOISE GATE – £405

◆ Settable to open/close via level (threshold) and via frequency
◆ Eliminates spurious triggering of gate by unwanted sounds
◆ Switchable from gating to ducking
◆ 1/4in jack inputs/outputs


## ALESIS MEQ 230 – GRAPHIC EQUALISER – £259

◆ Dual channel 30-band graphic EQ
◆ Independent in/out switches
◆ Independent master gain controls
◆ Independent signal-present and peak LEDs
◆ Jack and phono inputs and outputs

*Alesis MEQ230: dual channel 30-band graphic: jack and phono ins/outs*

*Drawmer DL241's auto functions minimise set-up time*

## YAMAHA REV100 – 16-bit digital reverb – £265

✦ Stereo inputs and outputs
✦ 99 high quality pre-programmed reverb and delay effects
✦ True stereo reverb programs
✦ MIDI compatible

## ALESIS MIDIVERB 4 – 16-bit linear PCM multi-effects processor – £399

✦ 200 programs inc reverb, gated & reverse reverb, chorus, delay, etc.
✦ Real-time MIDI control
✦ Multi-tap and stereo generation
✦ 85dB dynamic range
✦ 15kHz bandwidth
✦ Stereo inputs/outputs via 1/4in jacks

## DIGITECH STUDIO QUAD – 18-bit multi-effects processor – £499

✦ Four independent inputs and outputs (= two true stereo processors)
✦ Auto Input Levelling
✦ 200 programs inc reverbs, delays, choruses, pitch shifters, EQs etc.
✦ Large display
✦ Full MIDI implementation
✦ 22kHz bandwidth
✦ Uses S-DISC technology

## BEHRINGER DUALFEX EX2100 – variable sound enhancer – £149

✦ Variable Sound Processing circuit for increased brilliance and
transparency of high frequencies
✦ Fading between modes adapts the FX to respective program
material
✦ Automatic level control circuit to solve problems created by differing
input levels
✦ Available with jack or XLR connectors

*Yamaha REV 100: high quality pre-programmed reverb and delay*

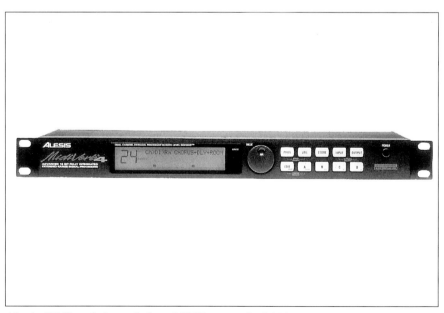

*Alesis Midiverb 4: real-time MIDI control of 200 programs*

## DBX 120XP – bass enhancer – £329

✦ Produces a new bass note exactly an octave below existing bass
✦ Gets the best from high-performance low frequency speaker systems
✦ Main outputs can be full range (including synthesis) or high frequency
✦ Separate subwoofer output with its own level control


## SPL VITALIZER – high quality sound enhancer – £433 (jack) / £586 (XLR)

✦ Utilises dynamic EQ, phase shift manipulation and harmonic filtering
✦ Unique feedback loop filtering system accentuates sub-bass without boominess
✦ Processing algorithms correlate phase and amplitude
✦ Choice of processing bass material either as tight, punchy sound or warm sound
✦ Independent harmonics control restores harmonics corrupted by recording process
✦ Stereo width expander can be used with psycho-acoustic EQ, or on its own.

# BACKLINE

You very possibly don't need me to say this (again), but backline is every bit as important as the actual instrument(s) you play. Just as a guitar's sound is a combination of every aspect of the design (things like the materials, the pickups, the strings and the setting-up), so every detail of the backline you use affects not only the sound you create, but even how you play your tunes. In fact, good backline isn't just important – it's vital.

We'll get down to the details in a moment, but the main thing about any backline is finding something that suits the music you make, and the way you want to make it. At its best, good backline will actually help you to make your music – and the good news is there are some pretty fine pieces of kit in town at prices that come close to being give-aways. The bad news, though, is you might well have to invest more than just a little time and effort in finding what works best for you.

Anyhow, let's take a look at the boring mechanicals, for which purpose, we'll start with...

## GUITAR AMPS –
## INPUTS, CHANNELS and EFFECTS

Down at base-level, an input is just a hole (usually jack-shaped) into which you stick the output from your, er, instrument. Most inputs can cope with anything from a low-output passive pickup through to the much-higher signal from, say, an effects pedal; there will usually be an input level control – this is the equivalent of a mixer's trim/gain control, and in itself has very little to do with the volume level you'll be pushing out. You can, in most cases, push the input gain far higher than might be technically ideal (whatever that means) and, depending on the amp, you'll probably get some interesting distortion effects.

But, by and large, creative distortion starts with the alternative inputs/channels many amps provide – these come in almost as many flavours as there are colours, with names like overdrive and crunch (subtle, eh?). They generally combine deliberate distortion with tone-shaping/EQ, and on some amps they're switchable effects rather than taking the form of separate channels. But switchable channels are more useful for most musicians, especially if this can be controlled by a footswitch (which it usually can), because you can then change instantly from a backing sound/volume to a bit of lead instrumentation.

Other effects, such as reverb and/or echo, may be built-in, or provided for by insert/effect loop sockets. As a matter of personal taste, I prefer outboard effects, simply because it's easier to choose an amp that gives the basic sound you want, then add effects to suit. Of course, you might prefer to use effect pedals rather than inserts/loops – there are no rights and wrongs here, so it's entirely a matter of how you want to work on stage.

## EQ

EQ is fairly fundamental to the job of customising an instrument amp's sound to suit both your musical intentions and the sonic character of the instrument you're using. At a superficial level, it might well seem that the more knobs, the better – but in practice, you soon discover that there's EQ, and then there's real EQ.

The point here is that just having a knob labelled bass, or mid, or treble, doesn't actually mean very much – it's how that knob works musically that matters. We could spend several pages exploring this, but the bottom line is that EQ design is a very special craft – which is why, for example, Rupert Neve (Focusrite) can successfully charge £2500+ for what appears to be a very simple box of tricks. When you're choosing an amp, spend as much time as you need to take the EQ thoroughly round the block, and if it doesn't work for you, don't buy it.

## POWER

If you haven't already read it, you'll find the basics back in *Power (And Some Other Imponderables)*. When it comes to backline, the key question is whether you'll be using your amp as the main means of getting your music through to the audience, or running it through a PA. In the former case, power is fairly important, because if you haven't got enough of it, people won't be able to hear what you're doing.

Most backline guitar amps are fairly modestly powered – typically 30-100 watts; if you're playing the pub/club scene, even 30-50 watts will generally do fine and, in my opinion at least, it's much more important

*The Marshall stack – JM60 shown here – is still a favourite of guitarists*

to find an amp that delivers the sound quality you want than get into wattish specmanship. This is especially true when you play with enough amps to discover that paper watts don't bear much resemblance to real-world loudness. To some extent, this is about things like speaker sensitivity (again, see *Power et cetera*), but though we haven't got the space to go into all the reasons why, it just happens to be true that some amps deliver not only more loudness, but also more of what matters musically, than others which may look better on paper.

Also, when you're checking out amps, watch out for those that only sound good when played at one particular volume and/or EQ setting, because unless you'll always be playing at said volume et cetera, it's not exactly a winning formula. Bear in mind too that volume levels can dramatically affect your ability to obtain sustain, though if you want to work at lowish levels, you can generally increase your sustainability simply by playing closer to the amp.

## TRANSISTORS and VALVES

The transistor is a magic little thing, simply because it's cheap, fairly reliable, and doesn't, contrary to what some people say, have to sound bad. But valve amps are still, for those lucky people with lots of cash, the only way to go – they're legendary for their warmth, their resonance, call it what you will, but they just seem to communicate more of what the musician is trying to say.

I don't think it's worth spending loads of space on this subject – if you can afford to think about valves, then you should most definitely take 'em for a spin, but if not, have a play with one or two anyway, and if you like their sonic flavour, it'll help you when it comes to choosing an affordable tranny amp. The main thing about valve gear is it needs love and affection to give of its best – there are piles of tech-type reasons for this (like the voltages that run them), but the bottom line is if you're going to use a valve amp, you should budget for an annual service check (probable cost £50-ish), keep a full set of spare valves with you, and know how to change them when the need arises. Easy they're not, beautiful they can be.

## SPEAKERS and CABINETS

A loudspeaker drive unit is a complex and subtle creature – far too complex to discuss in detail here. But what matters is that you don't allow yourself to be fooled into thinking paper specifications tell you anything worth knowing – they don't. The most obvious aspect of this is drive unit size, where there's a common assumption that for lead/rhythm guitars you need a 12-inch unit, and a 15 for bass. Cobblers. There are, in fact, a whole load of reasons why it makes more sense to use several smaller units – for example, allowing for real cone size as distinct from nominal size, four six-inch units have the same air-moving area as one 12-inch, and, all other things being equal, it's much easier to design a good small driver than a large one. Unfortunately, it's also a much more expensive proposition to manufacture, so you only tend to find multiple driver arrays on up-market cabs.

Any drive unit has a complex and subtle pile of interactions with the cabinet in which it's mounted. The actual material the cab is made from is more than marginally important, as is the way it's constructed, but it's also worth saying a few words about what's called the 'loading' it provides. As far as backline is concerned, there are three main types: open (or semi-open) back, reflex, and sealed box. You'll find more about these in the *Speakers* chapter, and all that really needs saying vis-a-vis backline is that, as with so many things, there are no theoretical rights and wrongs – if it sounds good in practice (ie capable of producing the tones you want), then good is what it is. Trust your ears.

## BASS AMPS

The most important points here are size, power, EQ and compression/limiting. Size-wise, it's perfectly possible to produce a good bass amp that's not particularly large, but in practice you'll generally find that big is better, especially at budget and mid-market prices.

Power-wise, bass amps almost always need at least twice the power of the lead guitar amp they'll be playing with – anything much less than 100 watts just ain't gonna hack it, even in quite small venues.

As for EQ, bass guitars generally seem to need much more flexible tone controls than lead/rhythm guitars, and a decent graphic EQ is a very useful item. If you have trouble getting a well-balanced sound across the full fret-range, or you can't get enough presence to cut through the rest of the band, then either dump the amp, or, if you like its basic sound, seriously consider finding the cash to put a decent 1/3rd octave or 30-band graphic in the effect loop (check out the Alesis MEQ230 – c£260).

Compression/limiting (see *Effects* chapter) can be very useful with basses, simply because, when correctly set up, they can effectively double the subjective power you've got.

## KEYBOARD AMPS

Just about the only thing that needs to be said on this one is that, unless you're using only a very limited range of voices, there's really no difference between a dedicated keyboard amp and a moderate-power full-range PA (with decent monitors), so check out both approaches before parting with the crinkly.

## DRUM AMPS

Rather like keyboard amps, except you need far more power – don't even think about anything under 300-ish watts. If you're taking it seriously, you might find that a separate PA mixer and power amp make more sense than a drum-specific amp.

## PRACTICE and STUDIO AMPS

Isn't 'practice' a wonderful name? Most times, what it means is cheap and, hopefully at least, cheerful. If you're genuinely going to be using it just for rehearsing at home, then power doesn't really matter, and even as little as 10-15 watts will be ample. But if you're aiming to use it as a cheapskate gigging amp, then you'll pretty definitely need something with a bit more balls.

Studio amps are very special items, and there aren't too many around. The most important aspect, other than getting one with a sound that suits your music, is that loudness isn't really important (apart maybe from its contribution to sustain), but *quietness* is – many gigging amps have very high levels of background noise/hum, and this is an absolute no-no if you'll be miking the amp for serious recording work.

*Some other examples of backline...*
*Top left: Roland's new KC-500 keyboard amp*
*Bottom left: Fender's recently restyled Squier practice amp*
*Right: Trace-Elliot's GP12/AH350SMX bass stack – available in bright red*

**119**

# FOLDBACK

As you'll probably have noticed at big-time gigs, the band often has two mixers: one behind the punters to control the front-of-house mix, and another 'in the wings' at the side of the stage. This second one is part of a totally separate system, supplying and controlling the stage-front monitors (or foldback), so each member of the band can hear what he/she wants from the mix via his/her stage monitor, and also get a general idea of the overall mix via 'side-fill' monitors, pointing in from the sides of the stage. Both the main and monitor mixers have their own sound engineer.

OK, why is it worth going to this much expense when it could all be controlled from just one desk? Some aspects of this will be discussed in *Mixing Part 2*, when we look at controlling the mix during a gig, but for now suffice to say it's not easy for a front-of-house engineer to control an onstage mix he/she can't hear, when the musicians are at the other side of a (hopefully) huge crowd of writhing, beer-swilling punters, with no means of communicating any dissatisfaction to said FOH engineer (except by raising the traditional two-fingered salute).

At some stage, the band invests in a new and bigger mixer for the main PA, then consigns the old one to foldback duties (sometimes doing the same with the engineer).

Having covered your (possible) future needs in foldback, we'll get back to the real world. For the average pub/club gig, you'll probably need just a couple of wedge monitors for vocalists and instrumentalists to share, and one for the drummist (this one can almost certainly never be loud enough). If you've only got vocals going through the PA, then that's what you'll hear through the monitors, and it'll probably be all you need (provided the bassist and drummer are near enough together to hear each other).

When starting out, you'll probably be happy with the entire band getting the same mix, but, if/when you start playing larger stages than yer average pub, and/or you've got so much dosh you don't know what to do with it, it makes sense to be able to give each bandmember a different mix (see Foldback Sends in *Mixers*, and *Mixing Part 1*). Do bear in mind, though, that separate mixes means separate power amps for each of them, so it can turn into quite an expensive hobby.

What amplifier(s) you need will, once again, be dependent on what sort of volume you want to produce – if you're running, say, 500 watts per side on the main PA, then a couple of hundred watts should easily be sufficient to provide all you need on the monitors. Don't forget, you're right on top of the monitor speakers, so you won't need mega-watts of power until you're playing really big stages.

Wedge monitors vary in size, but most are two-way designs with a 10, 12, or 15 inch bass/mid driver and a horn tweeter; powered versions are also available, which means you don't need separate monitor amps. Another way of avoiding separate amps is to use a direct feed from the PA speakers to a wedge monitor – but it'll need a built-in volume control, and you'll have to make sure it doesn't reduce the overall impedance to a level that threatens your amp (see *Power & All That Tech Stuff*). It does mean you get to hear exactly what's being delivered to the punters, and this can be considered a Good Thing.

You really need to go for the biggest drive unit you can afford, to start with, because on bigger gigs (should they happen along) you'll be less able to rely on the backline amps to give you an idea of what your bassist/guitarist/keyboardist is up to (assuming you want to know, that is). And if you've got decent sized monitors already, you won't need to buy (or hire) more.

Wedges are not easy to control, feedback-wise, because the speaker's pointing right at you. Side-fill monitors are usually similar speakers to those being used for the main PA, though not in the same quantity, and they are really useful on big gigs to give you an idea of the sound your audience is hearing. You can usually wind them up much more than the wedges without as many feedback problems.

Deciding how much foldback power you need is largely dependent on what sort of music you play – a gentle country or folk band will not be pushing out huge volumes, so will probably not need too much in the monitors to counter the backline; whereas a heavy metal band with stacks of 4 x 12in backline speakers will need high levels to hear what's going on (if indeed the band members are still capable of hearing). Many bands complain they just can't get enough level in their monitors (to the point where they expect to have the same sort of power from the monitors as for the main PA) – this is almost always a sign that the monitor mix(es) aren't being done properly.

I've already mentioned feedback, and will be doing so again in *Mixing Part 2*, but it's worth labouring the point that, no matter how directional a mike you're using, if you point it at a monitor speaker it will cause feedback/howlround. Also, the more directional it is, the greater the back sensitivity (see Hypercardioids in *Microphones*), so you have to be careful when moving about on stage. You also have to remember that, when you increase the overall gain, you could be increasing the monitor level as well if your foldback send(s) are post-fade, so use the monitor send control to decrease this by as near as possible an equivalent amount.

## IN-EAR MONITORING

One last word on the subject of foldback has to be about the recent phenomenon of in-ear personal monitoring systems – basically a fitted earpiece into which can have your own desired mix fed at the volume you want. You'll no doubt have seen lots of top bands using them on stage, or on the telly.

It's not a new idea: guitarist and ear-protection campaigner Jeff 'Skunk' Baxter was using specially-designed, spike-protected headphones on-stage with Seventies stars like the Doobie Brothers – he argued that wearing cans meant he could keep the monitoring volume way down and still hear everyone distinctly.

But it's become more refined and sophisticated in recent years: initially this meant the systems were hugely expensive, beyond the reach of all but the wealthiest pop stars. But the price is dropping all the time, and companies like Garwood have been leading the move into mid-price in-ear monitoring.

It's probably not an area where you can expect prices to come down to real budget levels, though, as there may be a temptation to cut corners on safety. Sound quality is important, of course, but if you're going to put any kind of speakers in your ears, you need to be sure they can't suddenly explode into deafening distortion – especially with the kind of power that's flowing around at gigs.

In-ear monitoring is something that will no doubt become more common, however, so look out for more information in *Making Music*.

*Jason Orange takes that in-ear direction with Garwood Radio Stations*

# SELECTED FOLDBACK

## EXAMPLES OF CURRENT MODELS

(This list is not intended to be comprehensive,
or to recommend some models above others)


### LANEY TM100 – two-way wedge monitor – £99 each

✦ 10in bass/mid driver and treble unit
✦ Power-handling: 65 watts
✦ Impedance: 8 ohms
✦ Size: 305mm (H) 440mm (W) 400mm (D)
✦ Finish: Black


### LANEY TM200 – two-way wedge monitor – £130

✦ 12in bass/mid driver and treble horn
✦ Power-handling: 100 watts
✦ Impedance: 8 ohms
✦ Size: 370mm (H) 450mm (W) 565mm (D)
✦ Finish: Black


### CARLSBRO ALPHA EM12 – two-way self-powered wedge monitor – £149

✦ 12in bass/mid driver and treble unit
✦ 100 watt power amplifier
✦ Volume control
✦ Size: 355mm (H) 505mm (W) 420mm (D)
✦ Finish: Black

*Carlsbro EM12 is a self-powered 100watt two-way monitor*

*Torque TM100 delivers 100 watts through a 12in driver and treble horn*

## TORQUE TM100 – two-way wedge monitor – £155

- ✦ 12in bass/mid driver and treble horn
- ✦ Power-handling: 100 watts
- ✦ Impedance: 8 ohms
- ✦ Size: 430mm (H) 580mm (W) 350mm (D)
- ✦ Finish: Black

## LANEY TM300 – two-way wedge monitor – £179

- ✦ 15in bass/mid driver and treble horn
- ✦ Power-handling: 150 watts
- ✦ Impedance: 8 ohms
- ✦ Size: 370mm (H) 585mm (W) 565mm (D)
- ✦ Finish: Black

## PEAVEY EUROSYS 1M – TWO-WAY WEDGE MONITOR – £180

+ 12in bass/mid driver and treble horn
+ Power-handling: 100 watts
+ Impedance: 8 ohms
+ Size: 380mm (H) 560mm (W) 400mm (D)
+ Finish: Black carpet

## CARLSBRO ALPHA M15 – TWO-WAY WEDGE MONITOR – £239

+ 15in bass/mid driver and treble horn
+ Power-handling: 200 watts
+ Impedance: 8 ohms
+ Size: 360mm (H) 670mm (W) 460mm (D)
+ Finish: Black

## TORQUE TM100P – TWO-WAY SELF-POWERED WEDGE MONITOR – £265

+ 12in bass/mid driver and treble horn
+ 120 watt power amplifier
+ Notch frequency, bass, mid and treble controls, plus HF defeat
+ Size: 430mm (H) 580mm (W) 350mm (D)
+ Finish: Black

## LANEY TM200P – TWO-WAY SELF-POWERED WEDGE MONITOR – £269

+ 12in bass/mid driver and treble horn
+ 120 watt power amplifier
+ Mike and line inputs, plus speaker, DI and headphone outputs
+ Size: 370mm (H) 585mm (W) 565mm (D)
+ Finish: Black

## CARLSBRO ALPHA PM12 – two-way self-powered wedge monitor – £289

- ✦ 12in bass/mid driver and treble unit
- ✦ 65 watt power amplifier
- ✦ Volume and input gain controls
- ✦ Six-band graphic equaliser
- ✦ Size: 355mm (H) 505mm (W) 420mm (D)
- ✦ Finish: Black

## PEAVEY EUROSYS 1PM – two-way self-powered wedge monitor – £294

- ✦ 12in bass/mid driver and treble horn
- ✦ 65 watt power amplifier
- ✦ External loudspeaker socket
- ✦ Mid-band notch filter/SCAN pot on input pre-amp reduces primary feedback
- ✦ Size: 380mm (H) 560mm (W) 400mm (D)
- ✦ Finish: Black carpet

## LANEY TM300P – two-way self-powered wedge monitor – £334

- ✦ 15in bass/mid driver and treble horn
- ✦ 150 watt power amplifier
- ✦ Mike and line inputs, plus speaker, DI and headphone outputs
- ✦ Size: 370mm (H) 690mm (W) 565mm (D)
- ✦ Finish: Black

*Laney's TM300P wedge monitor incorporates a 150 watt power amp*

# ACCESSORIES

Accessories may possibly not be the ideal name for this chapter, since it implies the items in question are some kind of minor optional extra – most of the time they're neither optional nor, in many cases, minor. Maybe we should call them "necessaries". Anyhow, here we go...

## MIKE STANDS

You might think mike stands are simple little numbers – a bit like the patrons of a pub, if they can stand up straight, they're OK. Afraid not: in my experience, every single cheap stand I've tried has been a complete pain in the posterior. It isn't that they don't stay where you put them – in most cases, they do – but getting them into that position in the first place is a very different story. This may not matter too much if you've only got a couple of vocal mikes to set up, but becomes more than marginally vital when you've got to rig ten or more boom stands (and the soundcheck starts in five minutes).

Rather than devote a couple of pages to covering every detail of stand design, I'll cut straight to the bottom line, and say you shouldn't be tempted to cheapskate: you need a stand where the base legs fold and unfold firmly, and the adjustable boom-arm allows you to take the counterweight well back from the stand proper, which is where many booms fall down (literally), when using heavy mikes. My own favourite is the Beyer GST500 (it also has the advantage of being black, which is less visually distracting onstage). At £55, though, it's nearly twice the price of some boom stands. It's worth taking the time to compare a few before you buy.

## CABLES and CONNECTORS

Like mike stands, cables turn out to be more complicated than they appear. There are three main aspects to consider: reliability, sound quality and flexibility. Reliability is the first and foremost requirement – even if you have spares, mid-show change-overs are not seen as the best way of impressing the punters. The wire itself isn't usually a problem, but poor-quality connectors and, particularly, the soldering, often are. If you have a choice, go for XLR plugs rather than less reliable jacks. If you must use jacks go for sturdier, metal-cased types, and keep them in good repair.

All cables have an effect on sound quality, but really good leads can be horrifically expensive (£50 a metre or more), and aren't usually practical for stage use as they tend to be what's called unscreened, which opens the door to hum and other interference pick-up. Curly cables (often incorrectly called coiled) aren't good news for sound quality, but if you're a guitarist who can't stand still, I have to admit they have their practical merits (not to mention their fashionable value during Seventies revivals).

Flexibility is most important for mike cables where the vocalist is moving around a lot, but also matters with static cables, as some types do their damnedest not to lie flat, so you either have to spend ages gaffer-taping them, or risk tripping over them.

Trying to keep things as simple as possible, I find the best approach to getting decent cables is, unfortunately, to throw money at the problem – anything much under £10 for five metres isn't likely to be worth owning: look for established brands like Klotz, Musiflex and VDC.

## DI BOXES

Direct injection/insertion boxes are a means of converting a high impedance instrument signal into a balanced low impedance signal your mixing desk can cope with. They come in two varieties – passive and active, and it's worthwhile going for the best you can afford, because in my experience, the cheapies don't work too well (a cheap transformer usually means hum and distortion). Active types are usually the best, and you can expect to pay £30+.

## STAGE-BOXES and SNAKES (MULTI-CORES)

These items only become relevant when you've got to the stage (ha) of having front-of-house mixing, by which time you'll presumably have a sound engineer who knows about these things.

But it's probably worth mentioning the basics, if only so you know

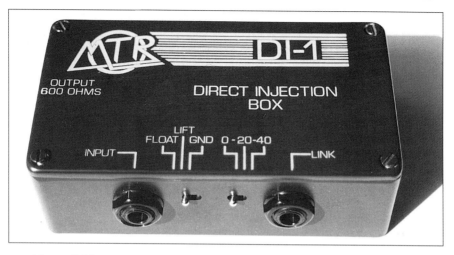

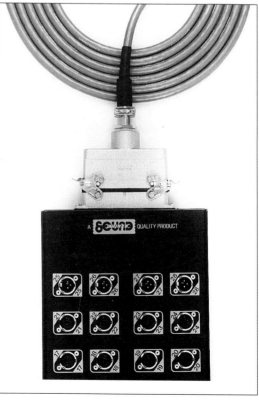

*Above: DI boxes convert instrument signals from high to low impedance for your mixer; passive and active versions are available*

*Right: in pro systems, stage boxes and multicores ('snakes') relay from stage to mixing desk everything you want to go through the PA*

what's going on when your engineerist presents you with an unexpectedly large bill.

A stage-box is simply a box you place on the stage (brilliant eh?),
containing a pile of sockets (usually XLRs), into which you plug everything that's going to be fed through the main PA; the snake is a multi-
core cable that carries the signals to the desk. The one utterly essential
point is to buy a stage-box and snake with several more lines than you
think you're ever likely to need — these things are renowned for dying at
inconvenient times, so spare lines may well turn out to be a show-saver.

## FLIGHTCASES

A flightcase may seem to be simply a very expensive suitcase, and
since 'very expensive' can easily mean several hundred pounds
(which may be more than the cost of the gear you're casing), you might
think flightcasing is a luxury you'd prefer not afford.

But... the fundamental point is that musical instruments and electronics are really quite fragile items, as indeed your musical career may
be, so, unless you're going to treat your gear with great respect (in the
Transit at two in the morning?), and your musical career with considerable disrespect, flightcasing makes a lot of sense. To put it another way,
if you take care of your equipment, it'll not only work better when you
need it, but it'll be worth more should you ever decided to sell it.

Using flightcases has further advantages: if you've got loads of
standard 19in rack kit, you can get everything into the venue far more
quickly if it's rigged up in one castor-fitted flightcase, than carting each
piece separately — plus you can have all the interconnect cables already,
er, interconnected, so we're looking at significant time-savings. (If you're
playing venues with stairs, get one of those handcart trolleys with three
wheels on each side.)

# BUILDING YOUR SYSTEM

If you're a solo artist, your choice is a fairly simple one: backline amp plus PA for vocals – PA for both instrument and vocals, or a combo instrument amp that does both jobs. It really depends on the type of venue you expect to play, and whether it's your intention to add more musicians at some point.

Chances are, if you're on your tod, you'll be using backing tracks, or, at the very least a drumbox, so you're going to need a channel for this, plus your vocals, and probably your instrument – but you do have a reasonably simple choice. A combo amp is certainly the cheapest option, but basic guitar combos probably won't do a very good job for bass drums or cymbals. If you've got the wherewithal, go for a mixer-amp plus speakers that will cope with more than you actually need right now (and bearing in mind that most cheap PA speakers are really only intended for vocals).

If you're in a band, you've got just two basic choices: backline plus vocal PA, or total PA, and your decision will probably be influenced somewhat by funds available (or, more realistically, lack of same).

You're looking for a combination of the right features, the right sound, and, most importantly, the right price. Your main concerns should be that you've got enough channels and adequate power for all the venues you're likely to play – features are important, but not quite so essential, and you should know a fair bit about what's got what, now you've read the product chapters.

Ideally, you should think about how your needs may increase if/when you start to play bigger venues; but as you'll probably only be able to scrape together the necessary cash for the system you need right now, just concentrate on getting the most comprehensive rig you can afford.

Trying out a PA system in your local music shop is about as much use as trying out a condom in the chemist. What you need to do is get the sytem into, as near as possible, your gigging environment (see *Creating Your Sound*). With a little friendly persuasion, you might be able to convince your dealer that 'sale or return' is the sensible route, and get him/her to give you a weekend, or preferably a whole week, to try the system out. This doesn't, unfortunately, mean you won't have to pay for it, but it will give you the opportunity to get the right system for your needs, with the minimum hassle. Don't forget, you'll have to treat the kit with respect and keep all the boxes et cetera, in case you do decide to return it – and expect your money back.

If you really can't persuade the dealer to part with the system on the above basis, don't try taking all your gear into the shop and setting it up – take along a CD player or cassette deck, plus representative-sounding CDs/tapes of your band, or a band whose sound you'd like to come near achieving, and play them through the PA system. This should give you a reasonable idea of its capabilities – though bear in mind that however low you set the volume, it'll sound pretty loud in the shop, so your test is for quality, not welly. You won't get a true idea of its output until you actually gig the system (see also *Power...*).

## BUYING SECOND-HAND

You might need to look out for a second-hand rig – after all, bands form and split up fairly frequently, so there's usually quite a bit about. It can also be the route to a real value-for-money deal.

Beware the battered and extremely old-looking system – no matter how cool or 'retro' it may look. If it looks knackered, it very possibly will be knackered, or certainly unreliable. Go for something that looks as though it's been treated reasonably well, and thoroughly check it out before you part with any money.

If you're buying from a dealer, ask for a six-month guarantee – you'll probably get three, but that should be long enough for any major horrors to rear their little heads. If you're buying privately, you've usually got next to no comeback, and you'll just have to rely on your instincts (and also make friends with a local service engineer).

For testing purposes, first thing to do is wire everything up and set your master fader(s) to somwehere near flat-out – without any input, for the moment, as you possibly don't want to frighten the neighbours with 500 watts of mains hum. Now have a good fiddle with every single knob in sight (now, now...).

Some hum, when you turn up the bass, is normal, and so is hiss at the top end, but neither should be too loud. The main area to look for nasty noises is in the fader s or rotary volume controls – crackling sounds

**134**

*One option is to go for a complete package from a single manufacturer*
*– like this JBL EON system, which includes JBL's own powered mixer*

from these will get worse as time goes by, and no matter how much of the ol' WD-40 you squirt into them, they won't get any better with ongoing use. Eventually you'll probably get dead spots, where there's no sound at all, and pots and faders are not particularly cheap to have replaced. Also check switches do actually switch.

Next, try sticking a mike through each channel, and making sure they all work – if there are some channels with line level input only, you'll have to use a guitar, or some other instrument.

Best test for the speakers is to use your trusty cassettte or CD player. Pump up the volume to the point of audible clipping (the sound suddenly goes nastily hard and raucous), check all drive units are working, and listen very carefully for any buzzing/rattling – if these are merely caused by a loose grille, or something similar, then all well and good (provided there are screws that can be tightened to stop it), otherwise, suspect that the old speaker voice coil is scraping against the magnet. This is Not A Good Thing, as you'll have to replace the driver immediately – if you still want to buy it, you'll need to take the cost of a replacement driver into account.

Haggling comes next; you obviously want the best deal you can get. If you aim to pay somewhere between 25 and 50 per cent of the new price, you won't go too far wrong, and the seller won't get ripped off. But, there's an old Latin phrase, 'caveat emptor', which I always thought had something to do with 'empty caves', but actually means 'buyer beware', or, 'if you're buying something, watch out you don't get stuffed'.

For one thing, with so many PA systems being bought on hire purchase/credit, you've got to be careful the gear is actually the seller's to sell, especially if you're buying privately – if he/she hasn't finished making the payments, it isn't. But he/she sure as hell isn't going to tell you, so the best you can do is get a receipt for your dosh. You'll also require it for the taxman if/when you earn enough to need to declare it.

## HIRING

The sensible route is usually to buy your own PA, because it works out cheaper in the long run – average nightly hire charge is roughly seven-and-a-half per cent of the new price, so you don't need an A-level in advanced calculus to work out that, after 14 hirings, that geat could have been yours. And you could maybe be doing a bit of hiring-out yourself...

On the other hand, there are reasons why regular hiring could make sense, not least of which may be that you simply haven't got the readies to buy a system, or perhaps you're not too sure how long the band is going to stay together. Also, if you're hiring, you don't have to be bothered so much about getting the kit fixed when it fails.

The occasions when you probably will need to hire are if/when you get the opportunity to play larger venues than usual, and your existing rig just isn't big enough to cope. This might mean an audience of 300 or more, for which you'll need around 1200 watts. For this sort of venue, you might be able to get away with using just a couple of mikes on the drums (bass drum and snare), but anything larger will require the whole kit to be miked (see next chapter).

If you do get to this stage, it's almost certainly a good idea to go for what's called 'wet' hire, which is where a sound engineer comes along as part of the deal. One of the reasons he/she will be there is to make sure his/her equipment is looked after, and doesn't disappear at the end of the gig. But he/she will (hopefully) know the kit well, and this makes for a fast set-up, an easy soundcheck for you, and a well-controlled mix during the gig (theoretically, at least).

Do check on insurance when you hire – is the gear covered by your policy, the hirer's policy, or the venue's policy? Also, what happens if the gear breaks down in the middle of the gig (or explodes, and burns the venue to the ground), or simply doesn't arrive at all – where's the compensation coming from? (Realistically, probably nowhere.)

You can find information on hire companies from books, such as *Showcase* (formerly *Kemps*) – your local library should have a copy – but most of the companies in here are big-timers; for anywhere much smaller than the Albert Hall, check *Making Music* classified ads, or talk with other bands, or your local music store, for people they can recommend. Word of mouth will definitely give you the best local deal, and the less distance the rig has to travel, the safer it will be – and it'll hopefully cost less, too.

# SECTION THREE
# CREATING YOUR SOUND

# MIKING UP

This chapter aims to help you get your microphones into the best position for miking all the players and singers your band is likely to have. You might have some weird and wonderful instruments that aren't mentioned – if you do, you'll have to play it by ear... as it were.

## VOCALS

Fairly straightforward. Bung the mike on a stand (boom stand if he/she also plays an instrument), pop it in front of him/her, and off you go (but do read the next chapter, *Mike Technique*). If you're using wireless mike systems, check out any areas where there may be a drop-out of signal and make sure your vocalist avoids them – it also helps to ensure you've got a new battery (and a spare) for your radio mike before every gig. If you hit feedback, it may be coming from the monitor rather than the main PA, in which case, move the mike, or the monitor (for more on curing feedback, see *Soundchecks* and *Mixing Pt 2*).

## BACKLINE

With guitar and keyboard amps, stick your mike on a short boom stand and aim it at an area between the centre and edge of one of the speakers. If you want a really bright sound, aim it at the centre of the cone, but never aim at the gap between two speakers – this doesn't work too well.

To DI or not to DI?. That is the question. Most sound engineers tend to DI (direct insert) bass and synths, and mike up everything else, but in cases where the bass guitar's tone relies on its interaction with its amp, it's quite usual to see miked-up bass amps. My own rule of thumb is, if it doesn't sound totally right DI'd, then mike it.

## ACOUSTIC GUITARS

Most modern acoustic guitars have built-in pickups, so they can be amplified by a backline amp or fed straight into the desk via a DI box (see *Accessories*). If your guitar hasn't got a pickup, or you're not happy with the DI sound, put a mike on a boom stand and point it towards the bridge from about six inches away. For a toppier sound, angle it more towards the neck, though you risk getting more handling /fret noise. If the guitarist moves about a lot, prepare for feedback in the low/mid frequencies.

Not many bands use acoustic bass, and the few in use often have built-in pickups. But, if you do have to mike one up, you need to get the mike as close as possible (and, if you can afford it, use a compressor/limiter). Once again, watch (or rather, listen) for feedback in the lower frequencies.

## STRINGS

Pretty much the same as for acoustic guitars – violinists do tend to wave their instruments around rather violently (hello, Vanessa Mae), so a clip/contact mike is probably a very sensible idea.

## PIANOS

Pianos can be Absolute Sods to mike. One way is to use a boom stand and position the mike over the strings somewhere between middle C and the top end. Don't forget to take the front panel off uprights first. If you've got plenty of mikes (and mixer channels) then use two, one near the bass end, one near the top, particularly if the piano is one of your main lead instruments.

Grand pianos generally sound best with their lids open, and often need two mikes – one halfway down the inside, and pointing towards the bass strings, the other in the middle, underneath the piano (seriously).

## BRASS and WIND

If you have a brass and/or wind section you can generally treat its members like vocalists and stick a mike in front of each of them on a straight or boom stand. If you've got a blowist who likes to roam around a lot while playing, stick a cardioid clip mike in the bell of the instrument, and, if you're really wealthy, a wireless transmitter on his/her belt.

## HARMONICA

Unless you already have a specialist mike for this, a vocal mike will do just fine (see *Microphones*). You'll have seen how most players cup their hands around the instrument and mike – this really does seem to enhance the tonal quality.

## DRUMS

Miking drums is an expensive hobby, simply because you're dealing not with one instrument, but many, and therefore you need lots of mikes. If you have a shortfall of mikes, mixer channels, and/or dosh, then the important things to mike individually are the bass drum and the snare, with one or two other mikes over the whole kit to pick up the rest. Good boom stands are a distinct advantage when miking drums, as you'll have to weave them between a forest of cymbal stands, et cetera.

Bass Drum – stick the mike on a short boom stand (a shock mount can be handy too), and position it centrally inside the drum. The tighter you want the bass sound, the closer you need to put the mike to the beater.

Snare Drum – position the mike at the rim of the drum, a couple of inches above it, and pointing towards the centre of the skin. If you put it any closer, the drummist will probably hit it and this is Not a Good Thing (it could damage the mike, or, if you're using an SM58, damage the drumstick). Alternatively, try miking from underneath – this gives a much deeper tone, though picks up even more snare buzz and rattle.

Toms – floor and rack toms should be treated in the same way as the snare, again being careful to keep the mikes out of range of flying sticks.

Hi-hats – your mike should be angled down towards the edge of the top cymbal. You can put it underneath, but you won't get such a good sound. Main thing is to keep the mike away from the gap between the two hats, which produces a big 'buh' effect whenever the hats close.

Other Cymbals – at small gigs, don't bother to mike these up at all.

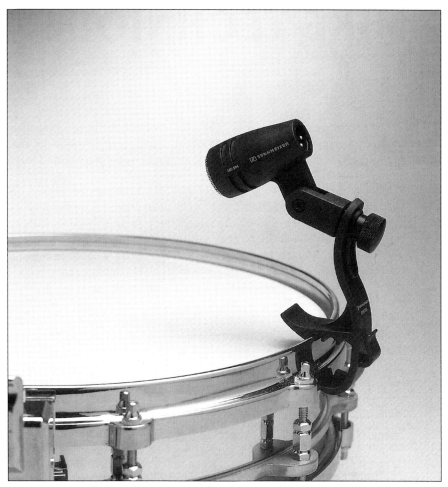

*An increasingly popular alternative to mounting drum mikes on stands is to use a clip-on system such as this one developed by Sennheiser*

They'll get picked up by the main drum mikes, and will probably be loud enough in their own right anyway. For bigger venues, use two mikes on boom arms, positioned about two feet above the cymbals, one roughly over the hi-hat, one over the floor tom.

If you're not happy with the results, experiment until you are, and be prepared to take a long time over getting things right (see *Mixing – Part 1*).

# MIKE TECHNIQUE

If you're a singer, whether lead or backing, the first thing to remember is that the microphone is your instrument, just as much as a guitar, saxophone or whatever, would be. Treat it as such, and spend time learning to use it properly.

The proximity effect (see *Microphones* chapter) can be a boon as well as a bind. You can add depth to your dulcet doodahs by getting up close, but you're also getting louder, so don't force it. In the same way, as you move away from the mike, you get quieter (obviously), and you can use this to control volume to great effect. Watch the way experienced vocalists deftly move 'off' and 'on' mike to match their own vocal dynamics. Don't expect the sound engineer to read your mind or react quickly enough to your vocal extremities.

The angle of the mike relative to the sound source is another factor that changes tonality and volume, so try out different positions to find what works best for your voice.

There is a point, just three inches away from the mike, where 'popping' and 'blasting' are worst, and this should be avoided as much as possible. Again, experiment.

Pop shields can be a bone of contention, and some say if your mike needs one, you should chuck the mike and buy a better one. But shields can have their uses, though even here you generally only get what you pay for: cheap ones at a couple of quid are just bits of thin foam, whereas the ten quid and upwards jobbies are made from specially developed acoustic foam, and they work.

If you're a drummist or keyboarder who also sings, you'll probably be contemplating, or already have, a head-worn mike. There's not much the user can do about these to change the sound, but for the best, and least poppy results, there's a half-inch rule – half an inch away from the side of the mouth and half an inch out from your face. Try it – it works.

Whether you stick your mike on a stand, or hold it, is largely a matter of personal taste, depending on how much you want to move around, and whether or not you're also playing an instrument. One thing to consider: if you want your fans to be able to see you, you won't achieve

*Otway guitarist Ronnie Carroll perfects his head-butt mike technique*

this by winding up the stand to above head height and having the mike pointing downwards, thereby obscuring your face. Conversely, if you have it too low, you'll be looking down all the time. In most cases, the ideal position is slightly below your oral orifice, enabling the punters to see said object in action. In the end, of course, it depends on your own style and the image you're trying to project.

While we're talking about image projection, don't forget that spot-lights (you never know what the future holds) reflect like mad off bright, shiny mikes, so choose one with a dark, matt finish (or get the black Hammerite out).

Radio mikes are extremely practical if you don't want to trip over your cables. When you do your soundcheck, take a tour round all the

**145**

*Play list? Melissa Etheridge demonstrates her unique slant on vocals*

areas you might walk (or fall) during the performance, and check for signal drop-out areas – if there are any, first try moving the receiver; if this doesn't work, you'll have to avoid these areas during the gig.

A similar but slightly different rule applies to very mobile vocalists with cabled mikes: use the soundcheck to look for trip problems, and make sure any perambulations won't result in up-ending the bass player, or falling a-over-t, and totally demolishing the drum kit.

Choosing a microphone that suits your voice and style is important. Try out as many as possible (see *Microphones* for a selection) and, if you've got several vocalists, you'll make mixing easier if you all opt for the same make and model, since the mixist only has to get to know the characteristics of one mike type.

# MIXING – PART 1

The first, and possibly most important, thing that needs to be said on this subject is that, unless you're deliberately setting out to be a clone/soundalike, you'll be well advised to create your own individual and unique sound – this is something that's primarily personal, musical stuff, therefore not this book's main territory, so I'll say no more...

Assuming you've got ideas for the kind of sound you'd like, the purpose of this chapter is to help you turn those ideas into reality, and the process starts with you investing some time in order to achieve this, before you even think about presenting your ditties to J Public Esq. In other words, as well as practising your songs, playing and singing, you need to practise getting your sounds right.

## WHERE TO DO IT

Any music/sounds/noise you make will be affected by the acoustics of the place you make them in – so it kind of makes sense not to use your spare room for this: apart from the fact that it'll probably annoy the neighbours, the acoustics will be nothing like those of a real venue (unless your spare bedroom happens to be a 200-seater with bar attached – in which case, I'll be delighted to pop round and help you with the job).

So, contact the manager/ess at a venue of the type you hope to play ("Hello, Wembley Arena – we're a new band, and we were wondering if you'd lend us your place for a couple of hours' rehearsal" – hmm...). Try local pub/club owners, or vicars, if you intend to play church halls – and be very nice to them, because they might just give you your first booking (well, maybe not the vicar if you're into death metal).

## WHO TO DO IT WITH

As well as all your kit you'll need someone to give an independent opinion on your sound. This is important, even if you have a long

**147**

enough lead (or a wireless system) to let you stand out front yourself and hear how everything sounds as you play. Ideally it should be a qualified sound engineer, but if this isn't possible, a friend whose opinion (and ears) you trust, and who's not afraid to give you bad news if needs be. Failing this, the aforesaid venue manager might be of help. Main thing is to find someone who's been to lots of gigs, and who can offer constructive advice, rather than just saying, "It doesn't sound quite right, but I'm not sure why". Such comments can lead to life sentences for manslaughter.

Big point here is to remember that you've got no punters present (which hopefully won't be the case at a gig), and punters, among other things, do tend to soak up the top end of the sound, which changes the acoustics of a venue quite dramatically. So you need to aim for a toppier sound than you actually want, and to add more reverb than on a real gig. If you can get your 'sound consultant' to come to a real gig too, he/she will (hopefully) be able to help you pinpoint the differences and make appropriate changes to the settings.

## HOW TO DO IT

First rule of thumb: whatever you're miking, fiddle with the mike position before fiddling with the EQ and if that doesn't work, fiddle again. Repositioning a microphone gives much more subtle and effective changes to sound than EQ can ever achieve. The ideal way is not to use the EQ at all – just have everything coming through flat. But here in the real world, compromise is what desk EQ is there for – after all else has failed.

Unless you've just pulled your brand-new instrument and amp out of their boxes, you should already know what settings deliver the sounds you like. Taking this as read, the next stage is to sort out the drums, if you're going to mike them at all (see *Miking Up* for positioning info). The first items to get right are the bass drum and the snare, in that order. Getting a tight sound on the bass drum is essential, otherwise it will boom/'bloom' over everything else, destroying rhythmic tightness. It also gives you a point of reference for all your other noises. Snare sound is more a matter of taste – you might like a lightweight piccolo sound, or perhaps prefer a big fat bottomy wallop (oo-er).

Bring up the bass and snare to around -6dB on the mixer and, once you're happy with them, bring in the rest of the kit, one item at a time,

*Think of your mixer as another instrument – practise with it to create your own particular sound*

until you've got the sound you want from the whole shebang. Now set your kit's internal balance – this is where multi-group mixers come in handy (see *Mixers*).

(It's common at gigs for the drums to sound bigger and better than everything else: while it's undeniable this can hold a live sound together (and grab an audience's attention), it often has a lot to do with the fact that sound engineers just love getting big drum sounds (it's very satisfying) and it might not always be appropriate to your music. Something to be aware of.)

Before you even think about the vocal mikes, sort everything in the rhythm section – bass guitar, keyboard bottom end, and so on. Start by bringing these up to about the same level as the bass drum and snare (but bearing in mind that if you've miked the rest of the kit, the total level will now be considerably higher than bass and snare alone).

Now you can set the vocal mike levels, starting with lead vocals, then adding backing vocals (if you have them). This part of your sound is very much up to you, because some bands like the vocals high in the mix, others like them almost inaudible – it's your music, so it's your choice; but you might be guided by factors like how good the singer is, and how strong the lyrics or melodies are.

Having set your internal balance again, you should now bring in any other support instruments (brass or whatever), and finally, after setting the old internal balance yet again, bring in any lead instruments which need to be heard above the others. If the guitar is important, for example, set its level while the vocalist is vocalling; also, if people are using different volume or effects settings at different times, work through them all.

Whether you're DIing or miking your backline, a similar rule applies to that for the drums – you should always make adjustments by repositioning the mike or tweaking the controls of the backline amp itself, before doing any adjustments at the desk.

Now you can start using your effects processor(s), if you have any, to subtly alter the overall mix, or individual parts of it (also see *Working With Effects*).

If you're using foldback, particularly with different mixes for each musician, spend as much time on these as you do on getting the main PA sound together. If you're in the happy position of using side-fills, these should be fed with the main PA mix, so the band can hear what the punters will be hearing.

Now's the point where you wake up that friend/lover/fan or whoever's going to be your objective sounding board, and ask for an opinion. Play two or three numbers at the settings you've already got and check how they sound. Get opinions from everyone onstage – remembering that, unless you're using side-fills, the friend out front has a much better idea than any bandmember as to how things really sound. But do be sure you've picked someone to make the final decisions – too much input from too many people can lead to compromises, and compromises can head you into Blandsville territory.

Once you've done all this, it's time to get out the Chinagraph pencils, pens, writing pads, et cetera, and make as many notes as possible. If you don't, you can bet your life you'll forget or lose some important setting next time. If it all seems like a lot of work, that's because it is, but it's time well spent, and every time you set up you'll find it makes life one hell of a lot easier – which increases the chances that you, and your punters, will enjoy the gig...

# WORKING WITH EFFECTS

The first thing is to get your effects hooked into your system. If you're new to the game, this can seem somewhat daunting, simply because there are so many ways of doing it – but there are really only a few fairly straightforward ground-rules.

If you want an effect on just one channel, you can either plumb it 'in-line' (between signal source and mixer), or use a channel insert (see *Mixers*). If you want an effect on several or all channels, either use an effect send, so different amounts of the effect can be had on different signals, or, if all signals are to receive the same treatment, either use a group insert or wire it 'out-line' (between mixer and power amp). Note that effect sends are totally unsuitable for effects where you don't mix the effected signal with the original signal – compressors and limiters are the main examples.

## LIMITERS and COMPRESSORS

The main controls here are ratio, threshold, attack and release. Ratio, as you might guess, determines how much compression the signal receives (the higher the figure the more the compression). If you're only putting vocals through your PA, then the style of your vocalist(s) will influence the setting you want – somewhere between 3:1 and 7:1 gives you an idea of the ballpark to experiment with.

If you're compressing the whole mix, your type of music will largely determine how much compression you'll want – gentle country or folk generally requires very little (unless you're playing in a very noisy environment), heavy metal will almost certainly need an awful lot more. The most important thing is not to grossly overdo it, since too much compression overall can make your music sound flat and lifeless.

Threshold lets you set the level at which compression kicks in, and below this level everything is left uncompressed. Take your time setting

*When using a compressor/limiter (such as this Alesis 3630), don't use an effec*

this – the main point is to ensure you're not getting any nasty noises coming up, particularly in the quieter moments.

Attack and release set the speeds at which the compressor kicks in after a signal goes over the threshold, and how long it stays in after it drops below the threshold again. Not too much fiddling here – if you get them wrong, you'll hear some nasty 'pumping' noises, and you'll lose the start and/or end of notes. In many situations it can be a good idea to opt for an auto compressor, which should adjust itself to avoid such problems.

## NOISE GATES

Fairly basic controls here: threshold (again), delay and rate. Threshold sets the signal level at which the gate opens and shuts, and a bit of wild twiddling will soon show you the settings to avoid – too low and you'll lose the end of every note, too high and your note will just go on for too long, and it'll let background noise through, so losing the whole point of having a noise gate in the first place. Aim for a happy compromise, probably somewhere near the middle of the knob's range.

Delay is rather like a compressor's attack control, determining how quickly the gate will open after the threshold is reached; rate is like release, setting the speed at which the gate shuts – you could think of these controls in terms of either slamming or gently opening and closing the gate. Choose a long delay and slow rate on things like vocals and a short delay with fast rate on snare and the like; somewhere in between on everything else, according to taste.

*end, as you won't be mixing the compressed sound with the original signal*

## REVERB and ECHO

You'll sometimes hear these described as "delay", but in PA terms, delay actually has a totally different application – only really relevant in large venues where, as well as the main on-stage PA speakers, you have other speakers way out in the crowd: a delay is used to ensure all the sounds reach the punters at the same time. (If you're doing a gig like this, you'll almost certainly either have your own sound engineer, or a house engineer, who should know all the settings required.)

Echo, as we've already discussed in *Effects*, is simple stuff – reverb is more complex; unless you're trying to emulate 1960s sounds, you're unlikely to want to buy a straight echo unit. We'll assume you've got a combined reverb and echo unit.

There'll be at least three controls. The first will be for input level, hopefully with at least a red overload LED – the simple rule is never to allow the signal to go into the red, because digital effects sound totally crappy if they're pushed above their maximum input levels (unlike some analogue stuff, where you might get a nice edgy distortion or interesting whacky effect).

Next, there'll be a program selector. There may well be hundreds of programs to choose from, so take your time making your selection, and make lots of notes of which program suits which number – bearing in mind that what suits one particular venue may be totally inappropriate in another. This is something to sort out when you're creating your sound.

Finally, there'll be a 'mix' control – if you're using your reverb through an effect send and return, you just wallop it right over to fully 'wet', and use the effect return level control for fine tuning; if you're using it between mixer and power amp, you have to fine-tune it to suit the sound you want. As a very, very rough guide, you might find that a setting around 10 or 11 o'clock is a good start. You'll probably find you need different 'mix' levels for different programs and different songs.

## ENHANCERS

I already mentioned the most important point about enhancers way back in *Effects* – don't use them on the overall mix, but only for one or maybe two elements you want to stand out.

There are no standard names for the controls on enhancers (partly because different enhancers have different features), but, whatever they're called on a specific model, the two basic controls enable you to determine how far down the frequency range (or up, in the case of bass enhancers) the beast operates, and how much new signal is generated (common labels are 'tune' and 'drive').

As with many effects, start with the controls somewhere around 12 o'clock, and experiment: for vocals, you'd probably set the tune control fairly high, while if you want to emphasise the breathiness of sax, you'd set tune well down into the mid-range.

Good enhancers can have almost unbelievably magical effects, but they do need very careful setting up, and overdoing things can make them sound almost unbelievably awful.

# USING SAMPLERS ON STAGE

David Anthony offers some notes on performing live with samples

There certainly are some amazing samplers around at the moment; internal effects of all kinds, analogue filters, not to mention truly elephantine memory. Unfortunately, lagging behind the cutting-edge users of any equipment revolution come the rest of us, too hard-up to afford the latest top-line gear, making do with the technological cast-offs... but producing the most interesting music, of course.

Using a sampler to maximum effect live – especially if it's one with a very limited memory – is an art unto itself, but a necessary one if you're a keyboard player: along with a sequencer it gives you the capacity for adjustment that a backing tape can't. There are plenty of purpose-built hardware sequencers which can take the rigours of touring, have no moving parts, and will not crash (famous last words).

When confronted with the sounds of an already-recorded track, the first thing to consider is which of them the audience will actually be able to hear at a gig. If there are any live instruments, eg guitar or drums, only the most essential/basic sounds will get through. Your supporting synth pads and delicately-tweaked sound effect details will just be so much noise cluttering up the venue's hard-pushed PA.

Some judicious EQing when actually sampling a sound can help the sonic picture no end. A rhythmical loop the drummer plays along with is often just needed as a background noise (as long as the drummer can hear it OK in the foldback/cans), so scoop out some of the main body of it, turning down some lower mid frequencies (roughly 400Hz to 1kHz) before sampling. A 'melody' sound intended to cut through a mix may benefit from extra high-mid frequencies (2kHz to 5kHz); while cutting any unnecessary bass will probably mean you can sample the business part at a higher level. And not all sounds need to be sampled at the highest bandwidth; some incidental vocal hits and noises sound better with a bit of lo-fi crunch to them – and you save memory too.

Once the sound is in the sampler, it can often be looped-up and still

155

*The popular Akai S range now includes the S2000, 3000XL and 3200XL*

give the same effect, especially if it's a more keyboard-type of thing. An organ sound is usually pretty easily looped – doing it immediately after any initial attack has finished means less memory used. Add a tiny touch of LFO oscillation to the volume (DCA filter) and possibly to the pitch, to simulate the Leslie cabinet picking up speed after two seconds or so.

A tambourine or shaker can help a groove no end, but sampled over a whole bar it eats up memory, so just take a couple of shakes and loop it, or – better still – program the sequencer to re-trigger it over the whole bar, at slightly varying velocities, and unquantised for the most realistic effect. And that drum or conga loop – is there a bit that repeats during the bar? Try looping it earlier to give the same overall effect – but with a shorter sound – and re-triggering it for each bar.

If you do have a drummer in the band, drum loops can be a slightly tricky subject. A regular old backbeat-type of sample might definitely have the groove, but that's what the drummer's for – and what's more, he or she usually does it with a physical power and intensity way beyond any sample.

What it nice, though, is the rusty old atmosphere of the loop; maybe you can find a suitable snatch of percussion with a similar sound, or try to recreate it by sampling with reverb. Sometimes adding a small amount of squashy, possibly de-tuned bass drum on the main beats, without too much attack, can reinforce the live bass drum without the drummer starting to feel redundant, and with no danger of flams.

Likewise, a bunch of handclaps on the main 'two' and 'four' snares – maybe with some (quieter) inaccurate ones among them – is a nice and vibey background to the hard snare crack. For some reason this all sounds best compiled into the same sample, rather than played individually by the sequencer – maybe it's because you put them through a compressor in the process.

Whatever sounds you use in the loop, whether it's a distant, incidental vocal yelp or something synth-based, think textural rather than copying what's already happening live.

For those of us with a sad lack of built-in effects in our sampler, there are ways around the problem without using loads of memory. A looped keyboard sound can be very convincingly phased by copying the sound, slightly de-tuning the copy, then putting both sounds in the same key. Experiment with amounts of de-tuning for speed of oscillation, and with negative or positive re-tuning for a downwards or upwards start to the cycle. Of course you only get one oscillation, but it sounds bloody great, and you re-trigger it when you need another.

Generally speaking, it's best to sample a sound with no effect on it (unless it's for a specific purpose, as mentioned before) because it'll be clearer in the live mix, and anyway the room will add its own reverb. But, if necessary, echoes can be added using the sequencer by copying the part to another track, drastically reducing the note velocity (assuming the sound is velocity-sensitive for volume) and off-setting the whole new track by the required amount to make the delay. Repeat this process with the delay track for more repeats.

Finally, when you've finished working on the whole set, play through it with the band and listen for samples that are too loud or those that are being lost, and adjust them accordingly (or possibly get rid of them). Then get hold of a competent sound engineer for an hour and play the sampler parts to him/her to check for any tonal problems – such as sounds that are just too piercing and trebly or overwhelmingly bass-heavy.

After all, if the front-of-house engineer isn't comfortable with the sounds, no-one's going to hear them anyway...

# BACKING TRACKS

Backing tracks can be a highly successful way of making your two-piece band sound like a four-piece, or your four-piece sound like a ten-piece. Or they can be a total disaster.

If your genre is programmed dance music, and most or all of your work dependent on machines, the main thing to say about playing live is beware of relying too heavily on software sequencing. Computers, hard disks and floppy disks might be fine in the studio, but they're notoriously unpredictable, not to mention incredibly vulnerable to damage, when you take them out on the road. Of course you have to do what your music demands, but if at all possible, use synths, samplers and drumboxes controlled by hardware sequencers rather than risk potentially disastrous computer crashes.

If your music's of a more traditional, non-programmed nature, you have to be even more careful in the use of backing tracks. Even though the phenomenon of 'personal appearances', where pop stars mime to a full taped backing, has been with us for some years, audiences expecting a 'live gig' may still feel cheated if they sense you're relying too much on pre-recorded assistance.

Many solo artists, of course, especially if they don't play an instrument, have to rely almost totally on their backing tracks; but for most bands the key rule lies in the name itself – don't be tempted to put any *lead* instruments/main vocals on the backing tracks, because the audience will wonder where the hell they're coming from, and then conclude you're cheating. But for putting in some backing keyboards, vocals, brass and so on, or maybe even an extra lead guitar line for the live guitarist to play against, a backing track can be the answer.

## WHERE TO DO IT

If your music includes some element of programming anyway, then, as we've said, it's just a matter of deciding which parts are to be played by which boxes, and making sure all your chosen sequences are going to be dependably reproduced on-stage. Take your set-up to a rehearsal room to try it out before you risk it for real at a gig.

If you're not into using sequencers live, but you've got a high-speed four-track and other suitable gear, you may be able to get away with the simple and cheap option of recording backing tapes at home. Then again, given the sound quality limitations of most cassette multi-trackers, and the volume at which the results will be played, this is only going to work for tracks that will be very low in the overall final mix.

More sensible by far is to work out beforehand exactly what you want on the backing, then go into a local eight-track studio. Unless you're doing something very complicated (and if your are, is it necessary?), you can reasonably expect to get through the tracks for three average songs in not much more than a day. So enough material to cover a two-hour gig shouldn't take more than about ten days – likely cost in the region of £500, allowing for a block-booking discount.

Things get worse if, as many bands do, you want enough material to be able to vary your playlist. On the other hand, if your backing tracks are only a couple of instruments, and you really do know what you're doing before you start, you could easily clear six songs a day.

## WHO TO DO IT WITH

Didn't we use these headings a couple of chapters ago? Anyhow, again assuming you're not into programming, if you want the backing tape to feature an instrument you, or another bandmember, can't play, you've got two choices: borrow a friend who can do it, or pay someone. In the first case, a few drinks should be a persuasive argument; in the latter instance, remember Musicians' Union session player rates are currently £80 for three hours – and from that you can only use 20 minutes of recorded music. Can you afford it?

If all else fails, a local music dealer should be able to put you on to someone who'll perhaps come to an acceptable compromise (some money *and* some drinks, maybe?). The main thing is to find a musician who either is, or can be, *empatico* with your musical style.

## WHAT TO PLAY IT ON

At last, an original heading... If you thought the idea of paying a studio, and maybe even a musician, was depressing enough, prepare for

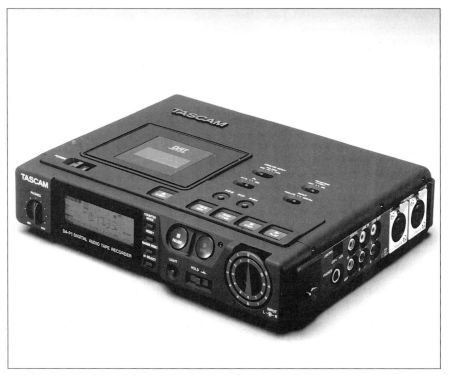

*DAT is fine on sound quality but search speed is too slow for a full set*

further Bad News. The thing is, although it would be nice (or at least cheap) to play the backing tracks on cassette, the sound quality isn't likely to hack it (for the same reasons that four-tracks aren't too hot); and cassette track-access time is hopelessly inconvenient for on-stage use, unless you make up a separate tape for every single permutation of your playlist.

DAT (Digital Audio Tape) will be fine on sound quality, but would only really be practical for the odd track, rather than a full set – its track-searching times are far better than cassette, but still not nearly fast enough for real-world gigging, when you've got an audience waiting for you to start the next song. And a DAT machine, at £400+, isn't financially funny either.

No, the only practical answer is CD-R (recordable CD). Now I'm not suggesting you actually go out and buy a CD-R recorder (though their cost has come down drastically in recent months – we believe you can get one now for under £1000), but there are plenty of companies who'll copy your master tape to CD for under £50 per hour's playing time.

The Good News is that the sound quality will be absolutely A1 (provided your original master is OK), and track access times are entirely fast enough. OK, we're talking dosh, but if you want to do the job properly, this is very definitely the way to do it.

Depending on the size of your repertoire, and bearing in mind that a CD holds a maximum of 74 minutes, you might want to get two or three discs made up, with say 20 tracks on each – they'd all include the "must-plays", with a different selection making up the rest of the set. You're looking at something like £250 for the CDs, plus £150 for a decent CD player (unless you've already got one).

## A FEW PRACTICAL POINTS

Unless you buy one of the very few (and very, very expensive) CD players with variable speed without pitch-shifting, you won't be able to vary the tempo of the song once the backing track's recorded.

Another point to note is that even if the backing only comes in for a few seconds in the middle or near the end of the song, you need to record the whole of the track, and a click (metronome) at the intro and throughout the track, then mix the foldback so the drummer and/or whoever starts the track will be able to hear it, so everything starts in-time and stays that way. This is vital.

You need to position the CD player next to someone who'll be together enough to remember to pause it at the end of each song, then get it cued for the next track (the track numbers should be on your playlist). As an alternative to track-skipping, you might program the running order into the player in advance, as long as you're only using the one CD (if you need to use more than one CD for a gig, look for a multi-CD player).

Finally, and Very Importantly, unless you're utterly positive that you'll be going straight from one song to the next in the CD's recorded order, and without any inter-track chat or retuning delays, it's a Very Good Idea to leave appropriate periods of silence at the end of each track (recorded onto the original DAT), to give the CD operator time to wake up, and do his/her job. Obvious common sense? Yes, but it's a bit late to discover this after you've spent £250 on mastering your CDs...

# SECTION THREE
# PRACTICAL GIGGING

# MAINS AND SAFETY

If you want to avoid Fried Musician Syndrome afflicting your band, it's not a bad idea to treat what comes out of that little wall socket in the corner of the venue with the respect (and fear) it deserves.

It's a subject I take rather seriously, so please, I urge you, read, learn, inwardly digest (whatever that means), and act on the contents of this chapter, even if you ignore everything else in the book.

## RESIDUAL CURRENT DETECTORS (RCDs)

The first thing to do is dole out your dosh (isn't it always) and get a residual current detector (sometimes known as an earth leakage trip). The cheapest of these are built like two-way adaptors (see below), and are mainly intended for use with electric lawnmowers and the like. They're better than nothing, but they suffer from all the soon-to-be-explained nasties of two-way adaptors, so it's well worth shelling out (a lot) extra and going for the in-line type.

But don't remotely imagine even the best residual current detector is a totally musician-proof means of preventing any kind of electrocution – it very definitely isn't.

## DISTRIBUTION and SINGLE SOCKET RUNNING

Mains electricity is distributed using what's called a three-phase system, and there's a potential variation of up to 415 volts on different phases. We don't need to bother about the technicalities – the bottom line is if you interconnect two items of kit running on different phases, your gear (and you) can end up as an unexpected and dramatic pyrotechnic display.

So, unless you've checked with the house electrician at the venue (if indeed they have one), it's essential you run everything off a single mains socket, and distribute power from there to all your kit, including front-of-house mixer and any recording equipment.

(I speak from personal experience here: I once had, understandably briefly, a summer job as service engineer at a language laboratory – I innocently, if idiotically, connected a video camera and monitor using sockets in two rooms only 20 feet apart. The subsequent explosions were extremely enlightening, as were the short Anglo-Saxon expletives used by the manager immediately prior to my premature departure...)

A single socket can run a surprising amount of kit: backline doesn't generally use much power (unless you happen to be Metallica), and can support at least 2000 watts of PA and monitors.

What you do have to be extremely careful about is if you also use your own lighting – this stuff eats power, so you'll probably need one or more extra sockets. Don't even think about connecting this to your audio system (for example, if you're running the lighting under MIDI control), until you've checked with someone who knows the electrics of the venue. And, if you're linking your kit to house lighting, again, check with the person who knows. (For more on lighting, see *Lighting*, naturally.)

Now, two-way plug-type adaptors: don't even consider using them, they're just not worth the risk. They're mechanically poor, so they can lose power at the slightest nudge, and they're electrically poor, so they may well heat up and can result in a special-effects display that wasn't on your playlist.

The best means of distributing power is via four-way distribution boards and if, as is very possible, you need two or more, plug one into the mains socket and then run up to four more from that board. When you buy said distribution boards, take off the covers and check the wires are securely screwed down (I've actually seen brand new ones where the wires had just been pushed into their holes, and the screws not screwed at all). Speaking of which, it makes sense to check your distribution boards and your mains plugs every three months or so.

A further word or two about mains plugs: it's not a Good Idea to go down the local market and buy 25p cheapies – they break very easily if dropped/stepped on, or are otherwise maltreated. More expensive by far, but much sturdier, are rubber-backed plugs – go for these.

Even distribution boards and rubber plugs aren't totally safe from the ol' Adnams Best Bitter, should bandperson, crewperson or punter-person decide to pour said murky nectar all over the stage. It's therefore a Good Idea to pop the boards inside plastic bin bags – it won't make them totally beer-proof, but will go a long way towards it. Better a bin bag than a body bag, I always say.

And please don't ever join mains cable by twisting the wires together and covering the join with insulting, sorry, insulating tape — this is a real invitation to Mr Sod to drop by, and it also happens to be illegal.

One final basic point: if one of your band should ever get electrocuted — usually recognisable by the sudden and unexpected cessation of musical contributions, and either a) complete absence of movement, or b) wild spasms of movement — do *not* try to yank said musician away from the guitar or whatever appears to be causing the problem. This is only going to result in you too becoming directly connected to the national grid.

It may seem pretty obvious to recommend that, as a matter of some urgency, you pull the plug on the entire system, but in some venues your kit may well be seriously obstructing access to the main mains switch. This is why I've listed rubber gloves (honestly) in *The Essential Toolkit*, because although it might take you a few seconds to don them (resisting the temptation to do any household chores), and only then yank the relevant cable from its socket, this may be quicker than groping around in the dark for a mains switch. Time won't be on your side.

## MAINS INTERFERENCE

If you're running computer-based equipment on stage, the last thing you want is a nasty spike of current causing your system to crash, so you'll need to get what's called a voltage filter. You should also seriously consider a UPS (uninterruptible power supply), which will keep your computer running for ten or more minutes in the event of mains failure — unfortunately, these beasties cost around £150.

Mains interference at a lot of venues is due to inadequate earthing — this will usually be evident when you take both hands away from steel-strung electric instruments and a hum can be heard from your amp. This isn't something you can do a hell of a lot about, other than running a secondary earth lead to a bloody great metal stake hammered into the ground.

## FUSES

Very important, even though small. Better they blow than you do. It's essential to carry spares of the correctly-rated value (see your equip-

*When you don't know about the phasing of the venue's electrical supply, there's only one safe policy – run all your kit (except lighting) off a single socket (as above), using a four-way distribution board like the one below, with up to four similar boards plugged into it*

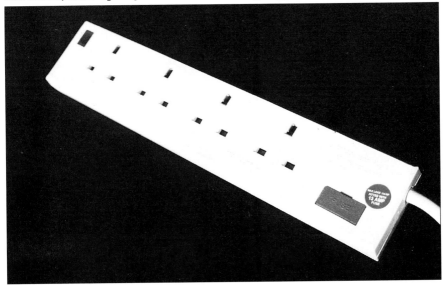

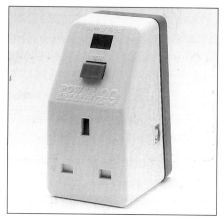

***Don't even consider using an adaptor (left) to distribute power***

***A residual current detector offers limited protection against shocks***

ment instructions). Six-inch nails, bits of tin foil or silver paper from fag packets may get your kit up and running again, but they might well also get you up and flying, literally – don't do it. Always use proper fuses.

Rather like light bulbs, fuses do occasionally give up the ghost without any particular reason (other than old age), but most of the time it's because you've done something to upset them. If a replacement blows as well, go to your Dealing With Disasters plans, while someone tries to find and fix the problem – if this doesn't work, either take a short evening course in electrickery, or hope there's a friendly senior electrical contracts manager in the audience.

## MARQUEES

Not the one-time great London music venue, but the sometimes great tented variety. Marquees are virtual necessities in this country during the summer months – totally open-air events have a tendency to result in drenched musicians and punters. But if you are playing in a marquee, take every bit as much care as you would at an open-air event with a thunderstorm threatening – humidity rockets in tents, particularly after a rain shower, so make sure everything's well covered.

Thoroughly check all your cables before the gig, and discard any with nicks, cuts or abrasions – wet grass makes a lovely earth, and you presumably don't want to end up six feet under it sooner than expected.

Find out in advance from the organiser(s) what mains supply (if any) has been laid on, and, if it's a generator, make sure it's going to supply enough current to meet your needs – as a rough guide, a 1000 watt rig draws about five amps at full power. It's also a Good Idea to check there's adequate earthing, though there's probably not much you can do about it if there isn't, other than go acoustic. The quality of generator-supplied mains power is not always very good (read, usually bloody awful), so you'll almost certainly need a filter for any computer-based equipment you may be using.

You might also want to take a look at the small print on your equipment insurance policy (you do have one... don't you?), and see if it covers you for open-air gigs – many don't, so you might want to get extra cover (or maybe just start insuring your gear).

## YET MORE ON SAFETY

This is a subject you'll find repeated throughout this book, because it's more than marginally material – you can't have too much good advice on it; or, for that matter, too much public liability insurance (in case someone in your audience meets with an accident during your gig – don't just assume your venue is covering you for this).

The main thing to bear in mind is that people are only human (well, some of them), and more than just a few were born clumsy: gaffer-tape all cables within tripping distance; make sure your tripod speaker stands are the sturdiest available (usually means most expensive), and be sure that, if they do fall over, they don't hit members of the audience – if you're daft enough to put them where they can land on you, well, at least you can't sue yourself.

Instrument stands (for guitars, brass etc) aren't just for show, or even tidiness sake. Gear left leaning against or perched on top of speakers/tables can all too easily fall or be knocked over – and they have a nasty habit of taking pints of beer with them, which can be both annoying and expensive (if not actually fatal).

Final safety nag – position all of your equipment where it's least likely to be knocked (in any sense) by punters. Not only does it make sense, but, if you feel safe, you'll be able to relax and enjoy the gig that much more. OK, that's the end of the health warning. (Until you get home, when you've got to remember to lock the door, shut the windows, unplug the telly, switch the fire off, brush your teeth... enough, enough.)

# PRE- AND POST-GIG STUFF

By and large, what most musicians want (when it comes to gigging) is simply to get on with it. Unfortunately though, the crude, rude mechanicals of physical reality tend to intrude, and the name of the game is therefore to understand them and know how to minimise their distractive potential.

As in so many things, it's just not practical to make hard and fast rules, simply because there are so many different band line-ups, hardware differences, and venues you might be working in. But here are a few guidelines, and it's up to you to decide which of them apply, or not, to your own particular situation...

## GETTING THERE

This is more than marginally material, since punters/fans, and managers/promoters, don't generally appreciate it much if you're not where you're supposed to be, when you're supposed to be. The main problem here is that most semi-pro musicians seem to have a dosh deficit when it comes to financing their transport arrangements (well, when it comes to financing almost anything), and though 15-year-old vans are great fun if you're into the joy of broken axles et cetera, they're arguably not the most reliable way of getting from A to B without detouring via garage Z.

So, if you do want to turn up on time, there are, boring though they may be, three rules: start out very, very early; always have at least two phone numbers of friends/taxi companies with sufficiently large estate cars; and never travel without a mobile phone (which are often free these days, when you sign up for one of the connection services).

OK, you can say the cost of hiring substitute transport could wipe out the putatively pathetic pennies you're being paid for the gig, but that's not really the point, which is that, in the long term, acquiring a

*170*

reputation for unreliability could be a fairly major negative asset.

By tradition, bands generally travel together, either in the legendary Transit, or in convoy in cars, and there's a lot to be said in favour of this, because if some kind of transport prob does wander along, there are more of you to sort it out. But if you're travelling separately, then back-up plans and mobile phones become especially relevant.

(If you're sitting wondering, 'Well how did people manage before mobile phones?', the answer is often very poorly. The technology's there now, so you may as well take advantage of it.) Whatever your chosen vehicle, make sure you've got adequate breakdown coverage, in case you're afflicted by something worse than a flat tyre.

## PACKING YOUR KIT

Maybe you're currently just slinging your amp and instruments in the back of your car, but once you get to the stage of vanning your hardware, there are two simple rules: pack your kit in reverse order to that in which you'll be taking it out for the set-up (last-in, first-out); also, as any pro roadie will confirm, 'tight is right'.

We'll cover set-up order in a mo, but the tight is right rule warrants a little elaboration. If you just stuff your gear into a van, it will rattle/bang around, which isn't widely-regarded as the best method of ensuring it arrives in working order. The tighter you pack all the bits, the less they can move around, and pros actually spend considerable time measuring every item, then figuring out the best way to get them in. (It's like a three-dimensional jigsaw, without a picture on the box to help you.) Since most semi-pro bands understandably don't generally flightcase everything, this isn't always the easiest game in town, but it's well worth taking seriously. If you're not flightcasing, you'll do the looks of your kit a favour if you cover each item with an old blanket (see charity shops/mum).

## SETTING UP

The easiest set-ups are at venues you play frequently, and if you've been in the game a while, you'll probably already know what set-up order works best for you. But on the assumption you'd like some ideas on achieving a quick, smooth set-up, here are a few general guidelines (they need interpretation, of course, since there's a slight difference between playing Wembley Arena and the Wembley Arms).

First thing to go in should be your mains systems (see *Mains And Safety*), so everybody can plug in and check their backline in time to find and fix any probs.

If you're running general PA, the mixer(s) should also go in early, so backline can hook up for test-plays and the soundcheck; and if you've got front-of-house mixing then lay in the stage-boxes and snakes.

Drum kits generally take far longer to set up than any other part of the hardware, so once you've established where your backline amps are going (normally either side of the kit), keep out of the drummist's way while he/she gets the hitty things together.

Then it's time to bring in the PA amps and speakers, followed by mike stands (if you've got quite a few of these, wrap them all in one or more old blankets/giant holdalls/second-hand golf bags even, so you can cart them in with the minimum number of trips).

Finally, bring in the guitars, keyboards etc (being sure to put these where they're not likely to get trampled on). By this point, you've humped all the heavyweight stuff, so you can start to pay attention to details, like the mike and DI cables, and finally, your mikes. All of these will travel most safely if you use ex-army munitions cases, not surprisingly available from army surplus stores (or see *Exchange & Mart*-type magazines).

Speaking of cables, it's important to keep signal cables well away from mains stuff, or you could end up with hummy troubles – this shouldn't generally be difficult, as you'll hopefully have laid all your mains at the back and sides of the stage.

Whether or not you choose to gaffer-tape your signal cables down is largely a matter of personal preference – from one viewpoint, gaffer tape can be a restrictive nuisance if you're going to be moving around lots as you perform, but if that's the case, gaffering the long non-moving runs can save you from tripping over those.

A reasonably happy alternative to spending ages gaffering is to use cable mats – though if you're running snakes to front-of-house mixing, serious gaffering is essential, because if someone else should trip over your anaconda, you could well be headed for legal proceedingsville, which might well get you some publicity, but isn't likely to do your bank balance any favours...

Excess cable should *never* be coiled up, as this creates a distinctly un-fun electrical phenomenon called inductance, which at the very least isn't going to do your sound quality any favours, and, in the case of speaker leads, could actually damage your power amp(s).

*Mains systems and backline should be first items into the venue*

## ROADIES

The *Concise Oxford Dictionary* defines a roadie as "a manager of itinerant musicians". Ignoring the word itinerant, I'd guess most musicians and roadies might be more than a little surprised by the term 'manager'. Hmm...

Anyhow, the key point is if you want to concentrate on music-making, then having a gear 'humper' can be a great boon: before the gig, it means you can leave most of the work to someone else, freeing you to concentrate on the really important things – like the beer, the groupies (ha), and maybe even your music. Just as importantly, after the gig, many musicians find they are, to put it delicately, totally shagged out, so having somebody to clear your kit makes more than a little sense, especially since you can then get back to aforesaid beer and groupies (if there are any of either left).

I do appreciate that most semi-pro bands aren't exactly making millions, but I also know quite a few people whose gigs pay no more than £80-100, yet find it well worth spending £20-ish on having a roadie. If you really can't afford it, maybe you can persuade a friend to help for free – at least at first – in return for a chance to share your glamorous lifestyle (?).

(Incidentally, it's interesting to note just how much roadies on major league tours can earn, which shows just how much they're valued – despite the old jokes.)

The main thing when it comes to finding and choosing a roadie is that, potentially, he/she can do a lot more than just lugging your kit in and out – a good roadie will also be able to handle most of the set-up details, like getting mike stand height right for each vocalist, and checking mixer settings are where they're supposed to be. Respect your roadie.


## STRIKING/BREAKING

No, nothing to do with industrial disputes, or physical violence, this is the craft of getting your kit out and, hopefully, back home in one piece (or as many pieces as it started out in). The whole process is obviously far faster than set-up, as it's largely just grip & rip/lift & shift stuff, but the packing order (assuming you're using a van), isn't necessarily the same as for arriving at a gig – if bandmembers want their gear to be dropped off with them, you pack to match the order they'll be staggering out of the Transit.

Given it's just remotely conceivable that one or more of the packers might have consumed a half-pint or 30 in the course of the evening, it makes sense to write down the desired order in advance, or at least have one responsible/together person in charge of the operation. ('Tight is right' refers to the packing, rather than the packers.)

In fact, it makes sense to have a list of items anyway, so you know you've not forgotten anything. Small items are especially easy to overlook, so you could store them all together in a case, with a contents list on the top. (If this sounds over-fussy, don't forget you may not be thinking straight in your post-gig adrenalised/knackered state.)

This is also a good place to point out that, sadly, if someone in your entourage doesn't keep an eye on your gear, it can disappear – from either inside or outside the venue. Obviously, the more portable (and valuable) the item, the more at risk it is, but it's not unknown for bass cabs and PA gear to be lifted. Thieves have vans too, remember.

*What do you mean, you thought I was bringing the mains cable?*

# SOUNDCHECKS

Ah, the joy of soundchecks. However much of a chore they may be, they are essential. It does rather tend to take the edge off your performance if you launch into the first number only to discover the lead singer's mike is dead/distorted, or not all your keyboards are coming through the PA. But it might be less than totally truthful to suggest most musicians find soundchecks anything other than a complete bore. Still, given their importance, it helps to know how to get through them with the minimum of hassle.

There are really three main aspects to the job: checking everything works; finding and fixing any technical probs (musical ones should have been sorted way before this stage); and making sure your mix balance is OK, not only in terms of getting the basic sound you like, but also how that sound is working in the particular venue.

Thing is, while it's certainly true that a basic soundcheck may only take a few minutes if everything is fine, it can take a long, long time if/when you do hit snags. And, in my experience, very few semi-pro bands (read, virtually none) allow remotely enough find & fix time. When, sooner or later, the inevitable problems do happen, it's usually blind-panicsville, because you're due to start your first set in two minutes.

This is especially true if you're playing the pub scene: for a start, few people really want to set up at five o'clock for an 8pm gig, then have to hang around for three hours: besides which, most pub managers don't appreciate bands making a pile of weird noises for hours before a gig – it tends to drive off early-arriving punters – so they'd ideally like your soundcheck to be over and done in not much more than ten seconds.

There isn't an easy answer to this one, but it's worth pointing out that, while there's probably not a lot you can do about it if you're only being booked to fill a wet Wednesday, if/when you're at the stage where your gig is a real punter-puller, and so a nice little earner for the venue management, you do have a certain amount of influence. If you explain that a ten-second soundcheck could well risk a two-hour silence later, and thus an even worse customer walk-out, maybe they'll see the sense of letting you do the job properly. You may have to do it much earlier than you'd like, though – which is good for allowing find & fix time, but you might have to fill several intervening hours if the check goes smoothly. (Explore the local shopping centre? Do a jigsaw of the Antarctic? Service the van, even?).

Once you get to the stage of playing larger venues (say 300+ people), it's more likely you'll cheerfully be allowed all the time you want to set and check – though this isn't a lot of help if you've got a day job to fit in as well.

But here's a scary little story: a friend of mine who does 'wet' (hands-on) PA hire was recently booked to do general PA for an R&B band in a 400 capacity hall. The system involved wasn't exactly in stadium-land, but involved about 15 mikes (ten on drums), 3000 watts of PA (2000 main, 1000 monitor), and eight main speaker cabs, with front-of-house mixing. The band had already set up all their kit, and there were two guys to handle the PA. They started at lunchtime, so you might think they were allowing plenty of cover for any probs. Hmm...

First, a drive unit in one of the bass cabs went down, which tied up one of the guys for about two hours, while he tried (unsuccessfully) to find and fix it. Then a mike cable died, which might seem like a simple substitution job, except that one of the stage box/snake lines also resigned, and since Sod's Law decreed it was the one the dead mike cable was using, it took quite a while to sort out.

Well, clearly, nothing else could go wrong. Hah. They finally brought the system up, and found that one of the 1000 watt amps wasn't amping (its LEDs insisted there was a signal when there wasn't; it seemed to be converting all its sound energy into heat). Take amp to pieces, run meter over it, find nothing obvious, take large dose of Mogadon. Then spend three hours phoning round for a replacement amp – no joy, so take second dose of Mogadon.

Come gig-time, the band had to work without one of the bass cabs, and entirely without monitors. Not a happy story – but if there's a moral, it's possibly that you should consider making all your music with just your voice and an acoustic guitar. You can understand why the Unplugged idea was so popular. (So long as you don't get laryngitis, or break a string.)

Still, down to practicalities...

# TEST-PLAYS

If you're running general PA, the first thing to do, after you've got everything set up, is ask everyone to keep quiet (if it's practical), slowly bring up the masters and channels to what you think will be a rightish level, and listen to the background noise. There's always going to be some, but if it's disturbingly loud (experience will teach you to tell), it's time to get to work. This is where mixer solo buttons and decent cans earn their keep – if you can't find the prob from soloing, then the nasties probably lie in your mixer-to-amp feed; or, if your mixer doesn't have effect solos, then just possibly in your effects system.

Now ask each bandmember to play just a single note/short riff or sing/speak into mikes; in the case of miked drum kits, drummists should only hit the bit of their kit closest to the mike in question. At this stage, you're only really interested in whether clean sound is coming through, and not so much about levels (unless they're way over/under, in which case take a look at your mixer settings).

Of course, it's just possible that nothing whatever is coming through on any channel, in which case the chances are either the power amp has died, or a speaker lead has short-circuited, blowing an amplifier fuse (or, just conceivably, you've forgotten to turn the power on – yes, it does happen). Naturally (?) you carry spare speaker cables and fuses, so it shouldn't take long to fix, but if the amp is genuinely dead then you're potentially in Deep Shit (see Dealing With Disasters in *Pleasing The Punters*).

On the assumption that your system has failed on either the background noise or clean sound tests, there are only a few possibilities: dud mike(s), duff cable(s), some kind of interference/hum pick-up, or misconnection at either source or mixer input. This last one is only really a candidate if you're simply not getting any sound through on one channel, while both mike and cable probs are checked by substituting another mike or cable – but remember that nasty I mentioned above: it's not unknown for, say, both a mike and a cable to fail at the same time.

Interference (usually in the form of buzzy noises) generally only rears its head in venues that have cheap triac/thyristor dimmers on their lighting. If it's only on one channel, try moving the cable round and/or substituting a spare. If these don't work, then you'll simply have to live with it (if it's bearable) or do without whatever bit of kit is giving the trouble (see Dealing With Disasters again).

Assuming you're right in thinking the fault's not with your system,

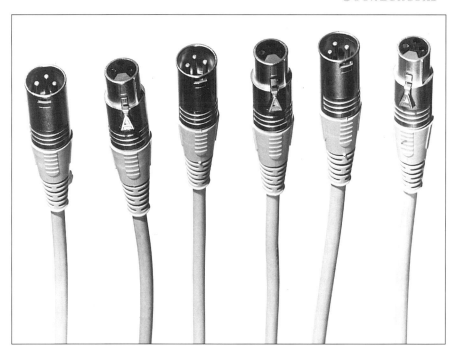

*Dodgy cables and connectors can be a source of hum and crackle*

you can give the management a bollocking for using crappy dimmers – on the other hand, if you want to play the place again, maybe save the bollocking and buy 'star-quad' cables, which, in principle at least, are the best for interference-rejection, if not really ideal for top sound quality.

Minor hum troubles are generally caused by mains and signal leads being too close together, but heavyweight hum is more likely to be the result of a really fun item called an earth loop. Without getting too techie (he said, immediately getting too techie), it usually happens because more than one item in your signal chain is connected to mains earth (yes, that green and yellow wire that goes to the top pin in the plug).

This is where some cures can literally kill. Professionals avoid earth loop problems because their kit is fitted with 'ground-lift' switches, an American jargon-term for a switch that disconnects the earth wire in the appropriate signal cable. Fine. But, as your gear possibly isn't in the true-pro league (yet), you probably don't have ground-lifters.

Time for a warning at this point – you may well hear of a fairly widely-used quick cure in these situations, but I have to point out there are some very, very, very important things to think about if you're tempted to try it. The dodgy practice in question is removing the earth wires from everything except one piece of kit in your system – normally the mixer (and even then only if everything is directly linked to the mixer, ie DI'd).

Trouble is, although everything will, in theory, still effectively be earthed through the earth side of the signal cables, this is only true if these leads are connected before ANY mains is turned on, and as long as the cables themselves (and a few other things) are working properly. If the slightest problem crops up, it could be Fried Guitarist time.

I must stress again, I would not recommend this technique at all – in fact I'm only mentioning it so you'll be aware of the fact that it happens, and that it's a very dangerous game to play. You'll no doubt come across people who'll say they've been doing it 'safely' for years – maybe they've just been lucky so far... Point made?

So what should you do if serious hum crops up? Assuming you've not had the prob at previous gigs, there aren't too many possibilities: either you've put something new into your system without checking everything out, in which case disconnect the offender and you'll just have to do without it (which serves you right for not checking it first); or you've got an equipment fault (all the more reason for not removing those earth leads). In either case, go to whichever of your Dealing With Disasters plans seems least inappropriate. After you've (hopefully) survived the gig, it's round to your dealer, and let a techie figure out what's going on before the next date.

## CHECKING THE MIX

In the good ol' days (or nights) bands used to run through one, sometimes two numbers, to make sure their mix balance was OK; but with the invention of the ten-second soundcheck, they'd need to be bloody short numbers. If you know that's the soundcheck time-frame you're working with, you need to figure out at rehearsals both how to pack the max into the min, and what you'll be listening for: you're looking for a quick 'snatch' (ideally based on something you'll be playing later) that lets you check overall balance, with guitarists using both lead and rhythm channels (if relevant), drummists hitting nearly everything in sight (on the kit, that is), and vocalists checking their lead/backing balance.

Yes, it's quite a trick to get all that into ten seconds, but it's also a trick well worth mastering: my own suggestion is to start out with lead vocals, then add backing harmonies, followed by a lead note and chord, then bring in rhythm and/or keyboards/other items, and finally drummy stuff.

If anything isn't right, the first place to look (assuming you've already done the solo test-plays described above) is at your mixer and/or backline settings, both of which, if you've followed the suggestions in *Creating Your Sound*, will be marked to show where you want them to be. If they're OK, then you're probably looking at a monitor balance or venue acoustics prob, and you'll find more thoughts on these in the next chapter.

One of the most common problems you're likely to hit is, of course, the dreaded feedback...

## FEEDBACK

An uncontrolled blast of feedback is just what you least want (though I have to admit it's a jolly effective way of getting the punters' attention). Obviously the first step towards fixing it is to find the cause – again, mixer solo switches can be a great help. In fact, it's often pretty clear where the source lies. Beware though: if you're running foldback it's perfectly possible to get feedback through the monitor system(s), yet think it's coming from the main PA. In this case, the first thing to do is to test-kill the foldback, to identify which part of your chain to look at in more detail.

There are basically only five approaches to fixing feedback nasties: move the source (mike); move the speaker(s); reduce the level of the offending source; play with the EQ; or use a pitch-shifter.

I have fairly strong views (what a surprise) on this subject, and they happen to be that, whenever possible, you should try to solve the prob by moving things and/or people around. In the case of lead vocal feedback, this may not be an obviously easy option, simply because very few lead singers want to end up standing behind the drum kit. But if it is his/her mike that's causing the feedback, it's time to look at the positioning and angling of the PA or foldback speakers – you'll quite often find that changing either or both of these by even just a few inches can make a quite remarkable difference.

If this doesn't work, you're potentially headed into real

*Testing, one, two... Eliminating feedback from vocal mikes is a priority*

Troublesville. Reducing level isn't really an attractive answer, because you presumably set the levels originally so they'd give the musical balance you wanted. So next comes the idea of using EQ to cure & kill – and there's quite a bit of territory to cover here.

Simple EQ systems, like five/seven-band graphics, are really of no use at all, because in the process of fixing the feedback, they'll also dramatically change the tonal balance of whatever's going through them. Something like a 30-band graphic is much more practical.

Here's an interesting thought: I recently watched a friend setting up a medium-size PA rig. After he'd got the system up and running, he took a high-quality mike out front, placed it about 20 feet away from the speakers, pushed the level (with nobody playing) until he hit feedback, then pulled the appropriate fader on his 30-band graphic. Then he pushed the level higher still, hit feedback again, and pulled another graphic fader. This went on for at least ten minutes, with at least 30 fader pulls.

At the time I thought what a brill technique it was, but afterwards I began to question it, because I thought what he was doing must surely be messing up the tonal balance of the band's sound. I later asked him about this, and he replied that most feedback problems (apart from obvious things like mikes being too close to speakers) are caused by the fact that speakers, and room-speaker interactions, have peaks in their frequency responses, and all he was doing was levelling them out. I'm not sure about the validity of the reasoning, but I must admit the final sound didn't in any way seem to suffer from the EQ work, so maybe it makes sense. If you have a large enough graphic, give it a try.

Another EQ technique, quite commonly employed by pros, is to bring in what's called a notch filter. This is a very narrow-band EQ cut control, affecting just a few hertz – but the trouble is those few hertz will almost certainly include the frequency of a fundamental guitar/keyboard/whatever note, and their effect on that frequency is much, much stronger than that of a graphic EQ. So you effectively lose the note at the frequency the notch filter is tuned to. Bottom line – I don't like 'em.

I also don't like pitch-shifters, because although the idea behind them is great in theory (you move or shift every sound up or down by just a few hertz, which effectively kills the feedback chain), in practice they often seem to mess the overall sound around in fairly undesirable ways. You'll find more on fighting feedback in *Mixing Part 2*.

# THE ESSENTIAL TOOLKIT

As we know, just about everything in life, except death and taxes, isn't remotely as reliable as it's made out to be, so it's maybe not a bad idea to plan for the inevitable cock-up.

What follows is a suggested list of items it makes sense to take to every gig. I've not included the kind of kit a pro engineer would need (like a soldering iron and a multimeter), because I rather doubt if most gigging musicians are going to want to mess about with such stuff at any time, let alone mid-gig.

Two practical aspects: there's not much point in having loads of spares and fix-it bits if you can't find them quickly in the stygian gloom of the Dog & Duck – so put everything in one of those multi-section toolboxes, label each compartment in big letters, and keep your torch on top of everything else. Also, there's not much point having them if you don't know what to do with said items. One example is fuses – in which case I suggest you draw rough sketches of your gear, with the fuseholders' locations clearly marked.

# THE LIST

*   spare strings (or pre-tuned guitar), picks, sticks and heads/skins
*   spare batteries
*   spare fuses of correct ratings and types (such as slow-blow or fast-blow – check manuals); at least ten of each
*   spare mains distribution board
*   spare cables (at least one of each type you use)
*   spare microphone
*   flathead and Philips screwdrivers to fit equipment screws (some gear has internal fusing)
*   spanners and/or pliers (for when your locknuts don't nutlock)
*   extra rolls of gaffer tape
*   torch (preferably including fluorescent tube – see Dealing With Disasters)
*   Elastoplasts (or maybe Band-Aids would be more apt)
*   fire extinguisher suitable for electrical fires (ie not watert) – try the small hand-held type sold for car use – anything beyond its scope, dial 999 and run like hell
*   industrial rubber gloves (no, I'm not joking, see *Mains And Safety*)

Other items, sometimes considered to be optional:

*   spare musician
*   electrician
*   emergency 24-pack of beer
*   Aspirin/Paracetamol/Mogadon
*   punters
*   groupie(s)
*   condom(s)
*   good luck charm

# MIXING – PART 2

The delights of mixing while singing and/or playing an instrument (or at least attempting to do same) can appear daunting even to the most confident of us (unless you happen to be one of the few people with six arms and two brains). But it's not quite as difficult as it sounds – provided you've carefully followed the suggestions in *Mixing Part 1* and *Soundchecks*, and have everything set up to your reasonable satisfaction.

The main thing to make sure of, during the first number, is that the vocals aren't being drowned out by the rest of the band – or indeed vice versa. You probably won't actually have a chance to do anything about the mix during the number, but listen carefully for any real highs and lows in volume, and/or any one instrument that's over-powered, or under-powered.

You may find it's useful to play the first couple of numbers without foldback – it can give you a much better idea of what the punters are hearing, which makes sensible adjustment much easier. Bear in mind though, that if you're on-stage, you'll either be to the side of, or behind, the main PA, so what you hear will be much less toppy than the noise hitting the punters.

Another point to remember is that, when you turn up the volume at the main channel gain control, it will also bring up the volume of any currently switched-on monitors (if you're using post-fade sends), so ease back on the send control(s). Conversely, of course, add to the monitor send if you're reducing the main gain.

Once you're happy with instrument levels in the mix – hopefully before you start your second number – it's time to listen to the overall sound. Too much low end can make you sound as though you're playing in an extremely large cardboard box; too much high will cut through to the back of the room with all the quality of a small transistor radio.

If that friend of yours, the one we discussed in *Mixing Part 1*, is still around, he/she should be able to help here, by taking a walk round the venue, and making sure the sound is well-balanced and (hopefully) much the same in all areas. Like everything else in life, practice makes perfect, and it may take a few gigs until you've gained enough experience to know what settings to use in different sorts of venues.

Don't start the gig with everything at full whack, as doing so leaves you without anywhere further to go as the gig progresses – save some headroom to increase the volume in your second set, when the place will (hopefully) have more, and maybe noisier, punters. (It's also easier for people's ears to adjust gradually to the desired volume, rather than be deafened from the start.)

## FRONT-OF-HOUSE

Front-of-house mixing means you'll have a dedicated engineer on the job (preferably just the job of mixing), and this is definitely the best way to do it – you won't catch Prince wandering off-stage to sort out his four-channel mixer.

Being at a front-of-house desk, of course, gives you the opportunity to hear the PA sound from the punter's angle, rather than how it sounds on stage, so you can start to consider the individual instruments and whether they're spot-on in the mix as the place fills up with punters (let's be positive here).

First the drums: you need to check you're keeping a nice tight rhythm (even if your drummist isn't), and the most important aspect of this is the bass drum. Don't let it start to boom – if this happens, ease off on the low end and boost the upper-mid. The snare should sound like a drum, not a tea chest, and a bit of diplomatic tweaking of the mid-range should result in the right sound if you didn't get it spot-on in the sound-check. Toms need to stay nice and bright when they're hit – keep the bottom end rolled off to stop them feeding back. Ride cymbals and hi-hat can be a right pain in the posterior – all you can really do is keep them fairly low in the mix, unless you need them for a particular effect, otherwise they can be overly distracting and get on your nerves. And if they're getting on your nerves imagine what they're doing to the punters...

Keep an ear on all aspects of the bass at all times – boom is bad, but too little bottom gives no foundation for the rest of the band. And if your bass player is the type that likes to put in lead breaks, you'll need to bring up the high end a bit to let the notes cut through.

Keyboard, rhythm guitar and such-like instruments can all too easily get lost in the mix: unless it's an obvious volume problem, use a bit of mid and top end boost to get them shining through again.

Lead instruments: the musicians behind them have an annoying habit of playing (or trying to play) solos, and unless they've got their own volume-boosting or channel switching completely sussed on-stage, you'll need to bring them up at the beginning of the fiddly-widdly bits, and back to normal when they've finished flaunting themselves.

Vocalists are probably the hardest part of the job, as they have a tendency to end up in just the spot where the mike will feed back. You have to be on your guard for the first sign of ringing, and suss whether it's from the monitors or the main PA. If you know your system well, and you've paid attention during the soundcheck, you should be able to get rid of it before it becomes a major problem. A little backing off at about 1kHz can work wonders. But, if you do get a nasty squeal, stay calm and think logically – don't ruin the whole mix trying to cure it. Be subtle. The audience is more likely to be perplexed by a drastic cut in volume/change of sound than a bit of howl (as long as it's short-lived).

The perfect mix is all things to all people: fans of the vocalist can hear every word, guitar freaks can hear every note, bass buffs can feel those riffs, et cetera. It takes work to achieve, and you've got to spend more of your time listening than twiddling. In fact, once you get good as a sound engineer, audiences may wonder why you're just standing/sitting/slumping there with a vacant expression on your face, and why you get paid for it. But you'll know...

## MONITORS

And hopefully the band will know, too. Musicians have a tendency to judge a sound engineer's capabilities by what's coming out of their monitors, which makes it a pretty important job, especially if the band are paying the engineer.

If you've done a good job of getting the monitor mix and levels right during the soundcheck, it shouldn't be too difficult to adjust them, bearing in mind any changes you're making to the overall mix – particularly if the monitor send is post fade (in which case be careful to back off in case of feedback).

A friend who does wet hire for local bands refuses to give them anything more than vocals in the monitors (mean sod). He reckons most of them don't use monitors anyway for their average pub gigs, so they're getting something new, and doing any more than that would just make his life at the mixer more complicated. So far, he's got away with it – but then he also hasn't had an invitation to mix U2...

If you've got (and I strongly recommend you do get) separate EQ for the monitors, you may be able to give the moaning musician a bit

*Musicians tend to judge a sound engineer by his/her monitor mix...*

more in his/her shell-like by easing back on the frequencies that were getting close to feeding back during the soundcheck (you did bring your notebook, didn't you?), and upping the monitor send volume. Most musicians aren't too fussed about the quality of the monitors' sound – they just like to hear what's going on at levels nobody in their right mind would want to tolerate. You'll know if the monitors are too loud – musicians have their own way of signalling this, usually by bleeding from the ears...

One more gigging hazard to watch out for is the 'alternative sound engineer'. If you haven't met him/her/it yet, you almost certainly soon will. He/she/it is a punter with a belly full of beer and a brain (?) full of helpful (?) ideas, who thinks that he/she/it could do your job just as well, if not better, than you do. And they won't go away. Once in a blue moon you might conceivably get a weeny bit of useful information, like, "The big box on the left isn't working". But mostly it's just opinionated, ill-informed twaddle about turning down the singer, or turning up the guitarist. The recommended approach is to make a few unintelligible grunting noises, pretend to perform some non-existent adjustments on an unused channel, and then tell your adviser it'll probably sound better now. (The point is it's pretty unlikely these people have any real or valuable experience themselves – if they did they'd realise how irritating it is for the engineer to be "advised" in this way...)

Having said all this, the most important thing about mixing is to keep practising, because you'll never know it all (none of us do). All you can hope for is that the audience, and the band, go away happy, and you go away satisfied you've done your best (and hopefully even been paid).

# LIGHTING

Tom Robinson offers a musician's overview of
how to light yourself simply and effectively onstage

Obviously, at mid-to-major venue level (2000+ capacity), professional lighting companies with up-to-the minute technology are needed to help put on a good show (computer-controlled 'intelligent luminaires', MIDI interfaces, all-in-one 'Golden Scan' units etc, have become the state-of-the-art norm). But for the rest of us, on a more limited budget, there are many times when it's better to get actively involved ourselves.

Yes, good lighting engineers are worth their weight in microchips, but the fact that someone can hump a few PAR cans into the back of a Transit van doesn't automatically turn them into a talented and imaginative lighting designer. How often have you watched gigs at pub and club level where the lighting was more of a distraction than an enhancement?

Lighting vitally affects the way your performance is perceived, and musicians should take a serious interest in how – and indeed whether – they're lit. There's no point working hard on visuals and delivery if every two seconds you're going to vanish in a lurid nightmare of flashing green and orange.

## THE BASIC RIG

Four lamps-a-side is the standard minimum rig most of us will need to deal with and, used properly, it can achieve an astonishing amount. It's cheap and doesn't require a genius to operate it, just reasonable common sense.

Each lamp consists of a black tin can (with, effectively, a car headlight stuck up one end of it) called a PAR can – PAR stands for Parabolic Aluminium Reflector. The PAR 64 is the most widely-used light fitting for live performances of any kind. They can be used white, or more commonly fitted with coloured filters/gels.

Bulbs for the PAR 64 come in two basic intensities: 500 and 1000

*191*

watts; 500 watt lamps are good because they won't fry your hair on small club stages; the advantage of 1000 watters is you can use deeper, more intense colours and still be seen – for instance, the staggering, electric, congo blue (from Lee Filters, no 181).

PAR cans are available in several different widths of beam (Raylight reflectors are often used for particularly accurate targeting), though with cheaper hired rigs it's a bit of a lottery which type you'll get on any given night.

## MAKING IT GEL

First off – and it may sound (ahem) blindingly obvious – check where the lamps are pointing. Get somebody to stand at each bandmember's stage position, and make sure at least some of the light from each side is catching them. Most PAR cans are actually directional, with a wide horizontal beam whose angle can be rotated by a porcelain mounting strip at the back of the bulb. So you can usually can climb up behind each lamp, with a heavy duty glove, and adjust the beam angle for maximum effect while aiming the lamp itself in the desired direction.

Backlighting (lights behind the band pointing into the audience) is a mainstay of conventional rock & roll illumination, and on large stages in big venues this will indeed create mood-enhancing beams of light. Try it in your local pub, though, and you'll blind the audience, while turning the band into silhouettes. Up to a point, there's nothing wrong with dazzling yourself on stage – it means you're definitely lit, and onlookers will never know you can't see them – but dazzling an audience for any length of time is simply daft.

Similarly, it may seem equally obvious, but check what colours are in your eight available lamps. Do you really want to be lemon yellow or violent mauve all evening? If the colours supplied with the rig are truly awful, it's much better to take them out altogether and use open white – which at least gives you good clean illumination. You can then vary intensities on your dimmer board to achieve changes in mood.

If you really get the bug, buy your own filters and take them around with you: nuances of colour are so emotive, and the gels are so cheap, that I'd warmly recommend this. The most widely used range are made by Lee Filters (01264 366245) who can supply samples of their whole range, while the gels themselves can be bought from Lighting Technology Group (0181 965 6800) among many others.

*Lighting vitally affects the way your performance is perceived*

## TACTICS

Keep the lighting appropriate to the size of the rig. At Wembley or Birmingham NEC you'll probably see lights flashing on and off every nanosecond, so it's a racing certainty that anyone with itchy fingers standing at your own dimmer board will flash those four faders up and down all through your set – it's what they're for, innit?

Watch while some other band gets this treatment. If it looks good to you, copy it... if it looks terrible, avoid. Remember the primary function of lighting is to illuminate – a fundamental truth that low-budget lighting 'engineers' all too often forget.

All this is easy enough to ensure if you're paying for the lights yourself, since any crew supplied with the rig will be working on your behalf. Often, though, some form of lighting will be supplied by the venue. This has the advantage of being free (hopefully), but the drawback that it may be very basic and in poor condition (especially the gels), and some local timeserver will have responsibility for it.

That person will want an easy life with a minimum of work and hassle each evening. All too often you run into the "we always do it this way" attitude – and you'll need all your tact and diplomacy to get this pitiful illumination adjusted to your own purposes and needs, rather than the local jobsworth's personal convenience.

## DISTRACTIONS

Two final visual thoughts: make sure the PA speakers don't obscure the audience's view of the stage more than they absolutely have to. Sound crews seldom give much consideration to visuals: contrary to what they'd have you believe, PA stacks can often be moved back to give a

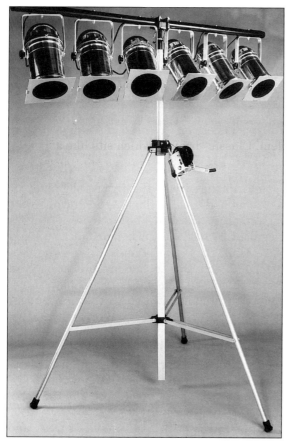

*If you're using a small portable rig of, say, half a dozen lamps, it's important to make sure those lamps have the right coloured gels. Otherwise you could end up bathed in lemon yellow all night...*

much wider, clearer view of the stage (and your wonderful lighting) without affecting the sound much. If they say this will cause feedback, experiment first by moving your microphone forward to see if they're right.

The other idea is to consider carrying your own black drapes around with you – basically cheap offcuts of cloth from your local department store. The smaller the venue, the bigger difference this will make, because of the amount of stray light that gets thrown around. With matt drapes over any gaffer-covered wallpaper and unsightly flightcases, extra light will be absorbed by the black material instead of distracting from your performance.

## SPECIAL EFFECTS

Paul Quinn looks at a few basic options...

**Smoke machines** – used to make a stage seem busier, or more atmospheric. Modern smoke machines are often actually 'steam' machines, heating water and glycol. Oil-based ones can't be used in small venues or where ventilation is a problem. Classic 'dry ice', which sits like a low fog on the stage, is actually quite difficult and expensive to get hold of.

**Strobes** – a mainstay of rave culture, can be effective on stage if used sparingly. There are also stipulations about the rate of the flashes, as they can induce epileptic fits.

**Mirror balls** – perhaps the oldest and simplest special effect of all, now largely limited to deliberately cheesy pastiche, though several mirror balls struck by lights (or lasers) can be unexpectedly stunning.

**Pyrotechnics** – explosions are always risky, but modern pyrotechnic gear tends to be safer than that of years gone by. Pyro stuff still needs to be treated with (professional) care, especially in smaller venues. Its use will usually have to be cleared with the local fire department, so make sure you sort it out a couple of weeks before the gig.

When using any special effects, it's best to check with the venue's management first, as there may be local safety regulations to consider.

# SUPPORT GIGS & HOUSE FACILITIES

These two subjects cover fairly similar territory – much of it to do with gigging etiquette, unwritten rules, and making your way in the big wide world of live work – so I'll tackle them both together.

Chances are the first time you'll get to use a biggish rig (unless you're absolutely rolling in it and have your own) will be when you play support to another (probably better-known) band; or if a promoter takes a chance on booking you into a larger than usual venue; or, of course, if you decide to experience the joys of bankruptcy by playing a major Pay To Play place (see below).

Venues that regularly book the big bands in your area will almost certainly have a house rig and their own sound engineer, and these rigs (not to mention the engineers) vary enormously in size and quality. I've come across fabulous custom speaker set-ups with really excellent mixing desks, but then I've also been to venues where somebody with less than a flair for DIY had decided a few chunks of chipboard and some ex-TV drive units would be adequate – and why buy a new mixer when you can pick up a really cheap second-hand one through *Exchange & Mart*, even if it does sound like a deep fat fryer.

Whatever the set-up, it might be your first (though hopefully not last) opportunity to have someone out-front mixing your sound. And so, whatever sort of a tosser you might think he/she is, it pays to get him/her on your side right from the start – uncontrolled feedback just when you don't want it can be very soul (and ear) destroying, and doesn't do much for the punters either.

Bribery and corruption rule, therefore – usually in the form of some free drinks for the engineer (preferably just enough to put you on a good footing, and not actually render him/her incapable). Talk to him/her about your sound, and how you normally achieve it. Take along notes of your own mixer settings, et cetera – they'll only act as a very rough guide, but the more info you've got, the easier it will be for the sound engineer to get your sound right (and most of them do like an easy life...).

**196**

If there's a foldback engineer, he/she is definitely a person you should go and get rip-roaringly (but not too rip-roaringly) drunk with, and make an attempt at immediate life-long friendship bonding.Generally, as a support band, being reasonable and organised will ensure more co-operation from the crew than being uppity and brattish.

## SMOOTH OPERATIONS

How long you get for a soundcheck will depend on the circumstances: if there are four bands booked for the night, or if people in the main band have taken an instant dislike to you or your band, then you can expect to have five minutes at most. On the other hand, if you're the only band, or you're friends with the main act, you might get 20 minutes to half-an-hour.

Before you start, make sure your backline amps are at the volumes you'll want them all the way through – whacking up the volume on your miked-up guitar amp half-way through the set is going to upset both the levels and the sound engineer.

It's unlikely there'll be a separate mixer for foldback in smaller venues, so you'll have to make sure you've got what you need while you're doing the soundcheck. Wild and desperate signals from musician to engineer during the gig can result in some extremely interesting mis-interpretations of meaning: a two-fingered return message from the engineer indicates you've upset said personage, and very probably won't get any more monitor level changes for the rest of the set; the sudden loss of all monitors, and departure of engineer to bar, means you've really upset him/her and, if you should ever be invited to play that venue again, you can confidently expect to enjoy an unbelievably crappy sound.

There are in fact certain conventions for indicating to the engineer how you would like things changed (assuming he/she is able to see them and willing to act on them): for example, if you want your own monitor level to be changed, point first at your monitor speaker, hold your hand out flat then either raise or lower it. If you want more or less of another musician's contribution in your monitor, point at your monitor, then the musician, then flat hand up or down. Also, assuming you've got side-fills, and you want a change in the main mix, point to side-fills, point to the musician you want changed, then hand up or down.

Beware about using this last one though, because unless the side-fills and your judgement are better than the engineer's, he/she may well

*Your first taste of a big system may be the house PA on a support gig*

know more than you about how things are sounding out front.

Lighting is also an important factor if you want to look good, as well as sound good, and the chances are that, in any venue with a capacity above about 400, there will be a lighting engineer looking after it. I know it's starting to sound expensive, but this is another candidate for the free drinks treatment. Talk to him/her about your music and what kind of lighting effects you think might help to enhance it in the punter's eyes. Again, though, once you've explained your basic requirements, don't be too demanding – at least at first. Perhaps even more than sound engineers, lighting people tend to like to do their own creative thing. (See *Lighting* chapter for more tips.)

## PLAYING THE GAME

It may sound prissy, but unless you're setting out to be totally anti-establishment, I do recommend respecting the rules of the house – if the management don't want you drinking or smoking on stage, then don't. And don't try playing big shot with the engineer(s), bar staff, or indeed anyone else – they've probably met musicians a lot more famous than you'll ever be, and they might just make an effort to remember you long enough to hold a grudge...

Having covered the house facilities, what if another band is sharing these with you? Well, the basic rule is much the same – get the engineer(s) on your side, or if not entirely on your side, at least not totally on the other band's. Although the 'crap sound and lights for the support band' syndrome is most common at major touring level where stakes are higher, it can happen anywhere, for a variety of reasons. I was at a gig recently where the resident engineer knew the main band really well – they were brilliantly mixed and had a full hour's soundcheck. The support band got all of ten minutes to check their sound, and a bloody awful mix as a result – throughout their set, the sound engineer was gazing into the eyes of his beloved. Someone from the other band, strangely enough...

The second thing to make sure of is that, while you don't get in the other band's way, they don't get in yours. Territorial disputes on stage can lead to very sick amplifiers, broken guitars, and even broken musicians, so avoid encroachment either way. Mark out your territory at the very start (lifting the leg and squirting is not ideal in polite circles), and stick to it. If you're just doing the first set, before the main band, then get your gear out of their way as quickly and quietly as you can, immediately you've finished playing (or else you may never see it again).

And if you should be lucky enough to go down better with the punters than the band you're supporting, don't get too smug about it – the same thing may happen to you in the not too distant future...

## BUY-ONS

It's worth briefly mentioning one of the harsh, economic realities of being a support band. If you do get a chance of second or third billing on a mid-to-major league tour, it's not at all unusual to be asked to "buy" your way on. As well as being expected to pay your own transport and accommodation costs, you (or your management/label) have to pay perhaps several thousand pounds to the headline act, as a kind of insurance/sweetener to help with their costs. With luck, you may be allowed to sell some of your merchandise at the gigs – one way a lot of bands recoup part of their touring expenses.

While we're on this uncomfortable subject, let's have a few words on...

## PAY TO PLAY

One of the less positive effects of the late 1970s punk era, with its have-a-go, anyone-can-start-a-band spirit, was that while musical energy levels undoubtedly rose, the quality of live performance became, how shall we say, less predictable. This meant your average, casual, walk-in-off-the-street gig-goer grew disinclined to take a chance – especially with the growth in home entertainment and multiplex cinemas as a safer and more comfortable distraction.

Soon it seemed – particularly in A&R-heavy London – there were more bands than there were audiences to go to see them. Not Good News for the live circuit. Inevitably, many gig promoters picked up on an easy way of giving unknown bands a chance to play while covering themselves against the possibility of no paying punters turning up. They'd ask the bands for money – hence 'Pay To Play' – calling it either a hire fee to cover in-house PA and lights, or a deposit that would be returned to the band if enough people came to see them.

Needless to say, while one can understand the theory, it's a system ripe for abuse. The Musicians' Union, who initially seemed unaware any musicians could even contemplate going along with such a scheme, eventually denounced it and began actively supporting non-Pay To Play venues. (If you want to find out their latest activities in this area, call the MU on 0171 582 5566. While you're there, and if you don't know already, ask what the Union's recommended minimum rates of pay are for live work, and see how yours match up: in theory a four-piece band should be getting at least £112 for a two-hour gig – and more if it's in London.)

The fact remains, though, that ever since The Beatles, and moreso since punk, there's been a huge glut of amateur bands playing 'original' material, expecting to be 'the next big thing' – and soon. They're often willing to put up with treatment and working conditions few professional musicians would tolerate, in the hope they'll attract: a) a bigger

*Being a support band can be tough*

audience, b) a rave review, or c) an A&R person's attention. And naturally there are lots of venues and promoters (and journalists) happy to service this market.

For all the talk of exploitation and rip-offs (which can't be denied or excused), this system has none the less produced some great bands. It's also produced a lot of under-talented, inexperienced, over-hyped mediocrity. Still, cause and effect can't really be proved – perhaps if the recent history of live music had been different, we'd be in a worse predicament. Who knows? One thing seems sure: the much-heralded death of live music is, thankfully, still a good distance away.

# PLEASING
# THE PUNTERS

So, you've got the sound you want (or as close as you're going to get until you can afford that nice £20,000 PA rig), you're familiar with all the kit you're using, and rehearsed to the point where your bandmembers very possibly can't stand the sight of each other any more. Now, assuming you're a totally unknown band, and you want to turn your noises into money, and/or public adulation, you've got to find an audience.

There are various ways of achieving this – other than bribing/emotionally blackmailing friends to keep turning up. One strategy is to visit all the local pubs/clubs that put on music and try persuading them you're the greatest punter-puller since Queen (either the band or the monarch), or Orbital (the band or the motorway).

If you decide to go this route, first check out the musical style(s) of the bands they already put on – it's in neither your interest nor the venue owner's to put you on if you're completely incompatible with their usual music policy – unless, of course, you can persuade them you'll bring enough people to make it worthwhile experimenting. Take along a copy of your best demo, and leave it for the promoter (with brief biog, gig listings, reviews if possible, and a 24-hour contact number – promoters often work strange hours).

An alternative approach some new bands try is to hire a local hall, then get their mates to charge people at the door (or go out onto the streets and drag them in by the short and curlies). This is not a stunt I recommend – if you haven't got to the point where local venues are booking you, how can you sensibly expect people who've never even heard of you, let alone actually heard you, to take a risk and pay good money to see you? Chances are you'll spend an entire evening discovering the reverberational qualities of an empty hall. And even if you manage to pack the place out with friends, you'll be very lucky to do this more than a couple of times before your audience dwindles (and with it perhaps your social success).

The object is to get yourself in front of as many punters as possible, preferably adding new ones each gig, and building a nucleus of fans who'll follow you, if not to the ends of the earth (remember to pack your Damarts for that Iceland gig), then at least to all your local shows. Once you've achieved this, and publicans/promoters know you're going to bring a pile of paying punters with you, you'll soon get regular bookings.

## WHAT TO PLAY/INVOLVING THE AUDIENCE

Probably the most important principle here is that although you have an absolute right to play whatever you want, the punters have an absolute right not to listen to it. This may sound totally obvious, but it's amazing how many bands who say they want to be successful willfully ignore it, and are deeply hurt when audiences don't respond to their every note. This doesn't mean you must only play lowest common denominator singalong standards, but just be aware that you're on a stage to entertain, not just amuse yourself. (The trick is to do both.)

Given this, it's vital you gauge how well each number goes down: clapping/cheering/booing/jeering/physical violence at the end of a song is only part of the story – watch the audience while you're actually playing each piece. You can't expect every single song to result in multiple orgasms. Very few people (that I've met, anyway) can climax continually for three hours. Recognising this leads us into the concept of...

## SETLISTS/PLAYLISTS

Most bands realise the importance of having a setlist – if not right from the beginning of their musical careers, then soon after the (regrettably) memorable incident when the drummist and the lead guitarist launch into the rock epic at precisely the same moment as the singer starts the first line of the smoochy ballad.

When you put together your basic playlist, bear in mind the point I made a moment ago, and don't try to go flat out all the way through your gig. The generally accepted formula is: first set – fast, slow, fast, slow, fast; second set – fast, slow, fast, go-to-bed. For sure, you can decide to do things differently, but the very fact that these standard formats are widely used kind of suggests they've been tried and tested over many years, so I for one am not inclined to try to fix what ain't believed to be broken.

Once you get to the stage of knowing the kind of crowd that's going to be at a particular gig, you can plan your setlist to suit, but until then, or at venues you haven't played before, I recommend having a minimum of three setlists: one is the core list (the stuff you'd really like to play, and using the formats suggested above); the second is to be used if you find the audience wants mostly fast numbers; and the third is if you suss the slowies are working best.

Another good idea is to start each set (especially the first), with a number you know your fans and friends really enjoy – their appreciation will help get the rest of the audience warmed up. You should also end each set with a 'strong' song (something with plenty of hooks and/or atmosphere).

## PRACTICAL PLAYING

One thing that makes good bands stand out from the also-rans is ending each number cleanly and tightly – no fiddly-twiddly bits going on and on because everyone wants to have the last word (or note). Good starts and finishes can make up for the odd sloppiness in the middle of songs.

And do say "thank you" to the punters – even if you don't think they're showing enough appreciation. It shows a degree of professionalism, and sometimes even makes them feel guilty enough to applaud the next number. Getting stroppy, or insulting an unresponsive audience (however tempting this may be) is not usually very constructive, and tends to backfire. Remember, there's almost always bound to be someone in an audience who likes what you're doing, so think about them and ignore the rest (if you can).

If you're playing your own material, and it's going down about as well as Madonna at a nuns' convention, there's always the option of sticking in a few covers of bankably popular numbers, preferably ones that get the punters singing/stomping their feet. This is assuming you're not ethically opposed to the idea of playing non-original material. On the positive side, playing covers you enjoy can be almost therapeutic – releasing tension in both players and listeners. (Even if you just play them in rehearsals, they can be musically educational too.) Then again, if you're trying to make a reputation as an original band, covers should only ever be an occasional diversion, otherwise you become known as, "The band that does the cover of blah blah...".

It's important for someone onstage to communicate with the audience between numbers – preferably, but not necessarily, the singer/front-person – even if it's just to announce the names of the songs. (Don't go into every single detail about how you wrote this on a wet Tuesday afternoon, and you'd just split up with the most gorgeous girl/boy you'd ever known, and your electricity was being cut off, and your dog had just died, and... Actually, that would make quite a good song...). Try singling out a couple of people in the audience to direct your comments at – eye contact can work wonders.

Most musicians are in the game for fun as well as profit – being realistic though, you can't sensibly expect every single gig to be a total stormer, and the point here is that the audience isn't paying to see you looking and sounding miserable (unless you happen to be Leonard Cohen), so try to get yourself into a positive frame of mind before you start. Decide beforehand that you're going to have a good time right from the start, and continue to do so thereafter, whatever may happen (well, maybe not if your power amp explodes and burns the venue down – though at least it will let you off having to do that tricky number with all the 13ths in it. Always look on the bright side...).

## USING SPACE AND LIGHTING

In the average pub you might reasonably ask, "What space?". An obvious point here is that there probably won't be many punters when you're setting up, so you may be able to do a little table and chair shifting. The main thing is that, however limited the space, you need to use it to your best advantage. As far as keeping up audience interest levels is concerned, moving around on-stage beats standing absolutely stock-still – for much the same reason most people enjoy watching television for longer than they'd stare at a still photograph. By the same token, most people prefer watching televisions with the brightness turned up at least a little, so wandering off into the darkest recesses of the stage is not recommended (unless of course the audience start throwing things at you).

Try to set up your gear so you have the maximum free space – there's no reason why a lead guitar amp can't go on top of a bass amp (unless the bass amp has top-mounted controls, or the combination is likely to fall over and break a tootsie).

Vocal PA speaker placement may need some consideration: you want to get your speakers up as high as possible – so the punters hear, rather than simply absorb, the treble – but you don't want them where they're going to get knocked over, or angled so feedback is likely. Speaking personally, I'd rather point them at the side-walls than have to mess about fighting feedback...

If you're doing your own sound, make sure your mixer/mixer-amp is where you can control it easily during the gig, and gaffer-tape any cables that could conceivably get involved with musicians' or punters' feet.

## DEALING WITH DISASTERS

Inexperienced people (and musicians) believe that Sod's Law says if a thing can go wrong it will. But real pros know the true version, which says even if something cannot possibly go wrong in a million years, it will anyway (ever seen a 300-seater marquee collapse and burn down in the middle of the second set?).

The main thing is to do some contingency planning, so you know what to do when Mr Sod walks up and kicks you where it hurts. Some of this is just plain obvious, like carrying spare strings, sticks and skins (that's as in drums, not for rolling up). Other predictable disasters include equipment failure, lighting failure, and total mains failure – the kind of incident most commonly caused by some genius knocking a pint of finest into your distribution boards.

(I was once at a gig where the bass drum beater broke, then the lead guitar amp went down, the snare head snapped, and finally the vocal mike died – I have to say what followed was one of the most fascinating renditions of "Pretty Woman" I have ever had the misfortune to experience. The bass guitarist was trying, less than wholly successfully, to play lead; the snare and bass drum beats were replaced with a variety of hastily improvised, if not entirely appropriate tom rolls; and the singer had to turn his back on the audience to use the guitar cab microphone...)

Anyhow, the practical point is to expect the unexpected. A stand-by battery-powered practice amp (ideally with a mike channel too) is a definite asset (though maybe not much use if you're playing Wembley Arena). You might also consider an acoustic guitar and/or battery-powered keyboard.

On the lighting front, a hand-lamp with a fluorescent tube will keep you at least faintly visible when the Bog and Bucket's sole spotlight dies. Another useful item, though not one that costs money, is a stock of

*If your audience looks like this, you're doing something right*

jokes (and the ability to tell them well), which will help fill in time while you put fresh batteries into your back-up amp, or tune the acoustic guitar.

If it's a matter of just one bit of equipment going down, you can cover this possibility by working out in advance exactly what to do. If the PA system dies, you've got your backline, and vice versa. Discuss and run through the procedure at rehearsals (but stop short of actually electrocuting the guitarist), so you can instantly spring into action when disaster strikes during a gig, and keep down-time to a minimum. You could prepare at least one number that can be done without each bandmember, to allow time for that person to sort out their gear, but avoid causing a complete break in the performance.

If lightning strikes the pub and kills everyone in it, including the entire band, this is (just about) considered an adequate excuse for ending the gig at that point. Then again, if even a single punter is left standing, he/she will give you a lousy posthumous reputation (and good old Mr Sod decrees that the single survivor will be a music journalist...).

In any event, the very best of luck (you'll almost certainly need it at one time or another). And above all, have fun.